Nkrumah and Nyerere:
How to unite Africa

Lawrence E. K. Lupalo

Nkrumah and Nyerere: How to unite Africa

First Edition

ISBN-13: 9781724755674
ISBN-10: 1724755676

CreateSpace
Scotts Valley, California, USA

Quest for Unity

KWAME NKRUMAH and Julius Nyerere were the most prominent African leaders who clearly outlined their vision for a united Africa and how to achieve it.

They also shared a belief in socialism but differed on how to pursue it as much as they differed on how to achieve African unity on a continental scale under one government.

Kwame Nkrumah stood out as a proponent of Marxism-Leninism. Nyerere pursued African socialism based on the African traditional way of life which he contended was basically socialist.

They were also deeply committed to the liberation of Africa.

Renowned Kenyan scholar, Professor Ali Mazrui, stated the following about Nkrumah in his article, "Nkrumah: The Leninist Czar," in *Transition*, a scholarly magazine published in Kampala, Uganda, in the sixties:

"Kwame Nkrumah's first important publication twenty years ago was inspired by Lenin's theory of imperialism. The publication came to be entitled *Towards Colonial Freedom*. Nkrumah's last publication in office is his new book, *Neo-Colonialism: The Last Stage of Imperialism*. That too owes its doctrinal inspiration to Lenin's theory of imperialism.

There is little doubt that, quite consciously, Nkrumah saw himself as an African Lenin. He wanted to go down in history as a major political theorist – and he wanted a particular stream of thought to bear his own name. Hence the term 'Nkrumahism' – a name for an ideology that he hoped would assume the same historic and revolutionary status as 'Leninism.' The fountainhead of both Nkrumahism and Leninism was to remain Marxism – but these two streams that flowed from Marx were to have a historic significance in their own right.

Like Lenin, Nkrumah created 'the Circle' – a group of friends to discuss ideas and formulate theories of revolution. Like Lenin, Nkrumah encouraged the emergence of a Marxist newspaper called *Spark*. It is true that *The Spark* in Ghana came to be more purist in its Marxism than Nkrumah himself. Nevertheless, the idea of such a newspaper was directly inspired by *Iskra* (Spark), the Marxist paper which was founded in 1901 through Lenin's initiative.

But while Nkrumah strove to be Africa's Lenin, he also sought to become Ghana's Czar. Nor is Nkrumah's Czarism necessarily 'the worse side' of his personality and behaviour. On the contrary, his Czarism could – in moderation – have mitigated some of the harshness of his Leninism. It is even arguable that a Leninist Czar was what a country like Ghana needed for a while.

Nkrumah's tragedy was a tragedy of *excess*, rather than of contradiction. He tried to be too much of a revolutionary monarch." – (Ali A. Mazrui, "Nkrumah: The Leninist Czar," *Transition*, Kampala, Uganda, 1966, p. 26).

Nkrumah also tried very hard to be acknowledged as a top-notch intellectual and as a philosopher instead of waiting to be accorded such status. Hence his claim to Nkrumahism that would immortalise him as one of the world's great political thinkers; unfortunately, he was not.

He tried to study for a doctorate in philosophy at the University of London but dropped out. His supervisor in the doctoral programme said Nkrumah was not really a philosopher and did not have an analytical mind.

He was just an average intellectual but very passionate, charismatic, dynamic, militant, daring, and outspoken on African and international affairs; attributes which, together with his forceful personality and oratorical skills, thrust him into the international spotlight and kept him there throughout his political career.

Nkrumah's Pan-Africanist mentor, C.L.R. James, in a letter he wrote to George Padmore in 1945 to introduce Nkrumah when Nkrumah moved to London where Padmore was living, bluntly stated: "He is not very bright." But he asked Padmore to help "this young man (who) is coming to you" because he "is determined to throw the Europeans out of Africa."

That is exactly what Nkrumah went on to do when he returned to the Gold Coast (Ghana) in 1947 after staying in London for about 2 years. He left the United States in May 1945 where he first went in 1935 to study at Lincoln University in Pennsylvania. As he stated in his autobiography about the ambition he had when he was still a student in the United States:

"My first duty is to return to Africa and join in the struggle for its liberation from the tentacles of colonialism."

He was deeply committed to the liberation of Africa and was continentalist in outlook even when he led the struggle for independence in his home country. When the Gold Coast won independence on 6 March 1957 and became Ghana, he declared:

"The independence of Ghana is meaningless unless it is linked up with the total liberation of Africa."

C.L.R. James and George Padmore were childhood friends in Trinidad (as Kenneth Kaunda and Simon Kapwewe were, in Chinsali, in the Northern Province, Northern Rhodesia). Both became giants in the Pan-African movement and enduring symbols of Pan-Africanism. C.L.R. James also taught Eric Williams in secondary school in Trinidad. Eric Williams became the first prime minister of Trinidad and Tobago after the island nation won independence from Britain in 1962.

C.L.R. James also wrote the following about Nkrumah:

"He used to talk a lot about imperialism and Leninism and export capital, and he used to talk a lot of nonsense." – (C.L. R. James, in Tony Martin, *The Pan-African Connection: From Slavery to Garvey and Beyond*, Dover, Massachusetts, USA: The Majority Press, 1983, p. 168. See also C.L. R. James, "Document: C.L.R. James on the Origins," *Radical America*, Vol. II, No. 4, July – August 1968, p. 26, cited by Tony Martin, "C.L.R. James and The Race/Class Question," p. 185).

He said basically the same thing about Jomo Kenyatta. In a lecture as late as 1973, C.L. R. James said the following about Kenyatta:

"At the time (in the 1940s), and even today, he was not very bright."

He also provided the context in which he made those remarks. In his lecture, "Reflections on Pan-Africanism," on 20 November 1973, in which he also talked about Kenyatta, C.L.R. James said the following about Nkrumah:

"Padmore decided to hold a conference in Manchester. He invited them all up and they came. By himself he could never have had that conference (the Fifth Pan-African Congress in 1945)....a very famous conference. At that conference there was Kenyatta, there was Nkrumah, and there was laid down at this conference the policy which Nkrumah carried out afterward in the Gold Coast.

Now I have to tell you how Nkrumah got in touch with Padmore and how that organization came to have these two men together. I was in the United States in 1941 and a member of my political organization came to me and told me:

'There is a young African here and he says he would like to see you.' I said, "Well, why should he say he would like to see me?' 'Well, I told him about you and he has read your book and I told him I could take him to see you and he said his name is Francis Nkrumah.'

So Nkrumah turned up, very neat, very graceful, very assured, he always has been, and we got together and we got to be friendly. And he spent two years with us. We used to go down to Lincoln University in Pennsylvania (where Nkrumah was a student), he would come up to New York and spend some time with us. We were very close until in 1943 (1945) he said he was going to England to study law and I wrote a letter, a letter that is famous in our annals.

I said, 'Dear George, there is a young African coming to England to study law. He is not very bright, but nevertheless he is determined to throw the imperialists out of Africa. Do what you can for him.'

George met him at Waterloo station and there began that combination. Now, why did I say that he was not very bright? Nkrumah used to talk about surplus value, capital instead of commodities. He had picked up these from some superficial quarters. He did not understand them really. About two years afterwards I saw Nkrumah and had read an article that he had written on Imperialism. He had learned from Padmore's extensive library and all sorts of papers and clippings. It was fully organized particularly in regard to the colonial policies of the African powers.

And Nkrumah was able to learn and was educated a great deal by Padmore. In addition to that, Nkrumah brought much creative energy and knowledge of Africa and instinctive political development which fortified Padmore and the two of them became a tremendous power together in the movement." – (C.L. R. James, "Reflections on Pan-Africanism," 20 November 1973, C.L. R. James Archive).

Nkrumah was not an original thinker, with an analytical mind like Nyerere and Senghor, although he obviously wanted people to think he was one. Nyerere never claimed such distinction even implicitly. It was the people, including his critics, who acknowledged his intellectual power. In fact, he made exactly the same point in a speech at a conference at Diamond Jubilee Hall in Dar es Salaam - the audience included foreign delegates - in 1970 in which he said don't tell people you are intelligent, or even imply you are; let other people say you are.

Even some of Nyerere's critics who also admired him because of his astonishing intelligence, high ethical standards, and commitment to African liberation and independence, said he surpassed Senghor in terms of intellectual capacity. As Jonathan Power, a British conservative, stated – when he wrote about Nyerere's high intellectual calibre – in his article, "Lament for Independent Africa's Greatest Leader":

"Measured against most of his peers, Jomo Kenyatta of Kenya, Kwame Nkrumah of Ghana, Ahmed Sekou Toure of Guinea, he towered above them. On the intellectual plane only the rather remote president of Senegal, the great poet and author of Negritude, Leopold Senghor, came close to him." – Jonathan Power, TFF Jonathan

Power Columns, "Lament for Independent Africa's Greatest Leader," London, 6 October 1999).

British journalist Trevor Grundy, another critic of Mwalimu Nyerere who once worked in Tanzania for a number of years, wrote the following about Nyerere's intellectual capacity:

"He went on to use his Edinburgh years to great advantage, bewildering - some might say bamboozling - liberal-minded journalists in the 1960s and 1970s with his formidable intellect....He had a blotting paper brain. Hardly a soul at Edinburgh guessed he would turn into Africa's number one brain box in years to come....Statesmen and journalists were amazed at his knowledge....The Rhodesian leader Ian Smith several times referred to Nyerere as Africa's 'evil genius.'"

Professor Mazrui, who said Nyerere was the most intellectual African leader, also stated the following in an interview with *The Gambia Echo*, 25 July 2008:

"The fact that Nkrumah had a greater positive impact on me than has any other leader does not necessarily mean that I admire Nkrumah the most. Intellectually, I admired Julius K. Nyerere of Tanzania higher than most politicians anywhere in the world. Nyerere and I also met more often over the years from 1967 to 1997 approximately."

Among African leaders, Nyerere was in a class by himself as a formidable intellectual, unlike Nkrumah.

There are also questions about the authorship of some of Nkrumah's works. The renowned Ghanaian philosopher, Dr. Willie Abraham who wrote *The Mind of Africa*, a highly acclaimed philosophical text, helped Nkrumah write some of his books, including *Consciencism:*

Philosophy and ideology for decolonization and development with particular reference to the African Revolution which was first published in April 1964, about two years before Nkrumah was overthrown in February 1966. In fact, he is the one who wrote the book. When the book first came out, there were whispers, right away, saying Dr. Willie Abraham was the one who wrote it; only to be confirmed later that he was indeed the one who did.

At the book's launch in Accra, Ghana, on 2 April 1964, and in Nkrumah's presence, Dr. Willie Abraham said among other things:

"Kwame Nkrumah has spoken time and again of the un-flowering of the African genius in conditions of independence. In this unflowering, he is himself making a contribution that is already astonishing. He has already proved himself a strategist, a thinker, and a statesman. Now, by his book *Consciencism*, he establishes himself firmly as a philosopher....In *Consciencism,* he has at length presented us with the matrix and theoretical sanction of his practice.

Consciencism opens with a discussion of philosophy. The author admits that it is possible to look at philosophy in diverse ways, but singles out two ways of treating it for extended development. The first which occupies the first chapter of the book is called by him the academic treatment. This, he says, arises from an attitude to philosophy as if there were 'nothing to them but statements standing in logical relation to one another.'

What this means is that the conclusions and the purpose of philosophical utterance are in this treatment made of less significance than the logical connections between the sentences. A whole philosophy can through being treated like this be made to hang in thin air having no connection with anything concrete or consequential. Philosophy thus becomes a kind of parlour-game, a mere intellectual   jousting.

To develop philosophy like this, Kwame Nkrumah could have used the plain historical method, moving from philosopher to philosopher. This would have been excessively laborious, repetitious and without much profit. His method was instead to identify the basic questions of philosophy, and to follow these questions through the characteristic treatment given to them by academic philosophy.

These questions are identified by Kwame Nkrumah as the question 'what there is' and the question how 'what there is' might be explained. If these are the basic questions of philosophy, then the answers to them must already determine the character of the entire philosophy of man. When such a claim is made, it is naturally needful to substantiate it. The claim gains substantiation in both the first and the fourth chapters; but especially in the fourth chapter where the author painstakingly shows how step by step his own answers to the two questions determine his ethical, political, and epistemological position.

Still developing the academic treatment, Kwame Nkrumah divides answers to the first question according to their treatment of matter. Those which accord to matter an absolute and independent existence, he groups together as materialism. And with this group he contrasts idealism.

Always going to the root of the matter, he avoids for the time being a headlong engagement with idealism, until he has identified its sources. These he finds in solipsism and in a theory of perception. He distinguishes two stages of solipsism, complete and incipient. I quote part of his discussion of complete solipsism:

'In complete solipsism the individual is identified with the universe. The universe comes to consist of the individual and his experience. And when we seek to inquire a little of what this gigantic individual who fills the universe is compounded, we are confronted with diverse degrees of incoherence. In solipsism, the individual starts from a depressing scepticism about the existence of other people and other things. While in the grip of this pessimism, he pleasantly ignores the fact that his own body is part of that external world, that he sees and touches his own body in exactly the same sense that he sees and touches any other body. If other bodies are only portions of the individual's experience, then by the same magic he must disincarnate himself. In this way, the individual's role as the centre of solipsism begins to wobble seriously, he is no longer the peg on which the universe hangs, the hub around which it revolves. Solipsism begins to shed its focal point for the universe. The individual begins to coalesce with his own experience. The individual as a subject, the sufferer and enjoyer of experience, melts away, and we are left with unattached experience.'

This passage is one of many which illustrate the author's succinctness of expression and vividness of thought. It is from this combination added to the accuracy of exposition and cogency of argument that consciencism derives its power.

Incipient solipsism is illustrated from the philosophy of Descartes. Kwame Nkrumah argues that when Descartes proposes to doubt everything that could be known through the senses or through reasoning, because both avenues of knowledge are full of pit-falls, and decides that he who is busy doubting things must exist in order to doubt, and therefore claims to exist, he claims too much. And now I quote:

'Though Descartes is entitled to say: *Cogito, ergo sum* — 'I think therefore I exist' — he would clearly be understanding too much if he understood from this that some object existed, let alone Monsieur Descartes existed. All that is indubitable in the first section of Descartes' statement is that there is thinking. The first person is in that statement no more than the subject of a verb, with no more connotation of an object than there is in the anticipatory 'it' of the sentence 'It is raining.' The pronoun in this sentence is a mere subject of a sentence, and does not refer to any object or group of objects which is raining. 'It' in that sentence does not stand for anything. It is a quack pronoun.

And so once again we have unattached experience, thinking without an object which thinks.

And as the subject is merely grammatical, it cannot serve as a genuine principle of collection of thoughts which will mark one batch of thoughts as belonging to one person rather than another...'

Discussing the other source of solipsism, Kwame Nkrumah writes:

'It is more normal to found idealism upon some theory of perception. Here, the idealist holds that we only know of the external world through perception; and if matter be held to be constitutive of the external world, then we only know of matter through perception. Quite gratuitously, the conclusion is drawn that matter owes its existence to perception. Granted that perception is a function of the mind or spirit, matter ends up depending on spirit for its existence.'

The author goes on to point out that the conception of perception involved is one which takes place by agency of our senses. And as our bodies are themselves parts of the external world, if body, being matter, exists only through perceptual knowledge, 'it could not at the same time be the means to that knowledge; it could not be the avenue to perception'....

Kwame Nkrumah does not content himself with attacking idealism at its roots. He also seeks to establish that idealism is jejune; that it cannot explain anything, and that it is incompatible with science and the existence of ordinary things like apples and oranges. His reason is that the idealists dismantle the world, and find that they cannot put it together again....

There are two aspects of the philosophical materialism of *Consciencism*. In its first aspect, it is a combative theory, seeking to destroy philosophical idealism to which it stands opposed. In its second aspect, it is ampliative. It seeks to give a general philosophical account of the world in exactly the same way as idealism is ampliative. Hence *Consciencism* not merely denies the theses of idealism: it substitutes for them its own theses.

Consciencism describes idealism variously as 'intoxicated speculation' and 'the ecstasy of intellectualism.'

In contrast, materialism is sober philosophy. The initial theses of materialism, according to *Consciencism*, are first the absolute and independent existence of matter; and second the assertion of the capacity of matter for spontaneous self-motion. And yet *Consciencism* criticises materialism"....

Dr. Willie Abraham was talking about himself, and about his own book, not about Nkrumah and Nkrumah's book. Excerpts from *Consciencism* make that clear.

Those who knew Nkrumah well knew, right away, that was not even his language and reasoning. He was not known for such philosophical profundity like Dr. Willie Abraham. That was not even his writing style. There is a big difference between the excerpts above – from the book, *Consciencism* - and Nkrumah's own writings in terms of style, substance, and reasoning.

If Nkrumah had a reputation for such intellectual depth, he definitely would have been able to formulate his own philosophy and ideology, based on his own original ideas, instead of relying on Marxism-Leninism as the basis for Nkrumahism – which was no more than an African name for scientific socialism, the intellectual product of Karl Marx more than anybody else – in a futile attempt to indiginise or Africanise Marxism.

Simply known as the mighty Abraham in some circles because of his formidable intellect, Dr. Willie Abraham was very close to Nkrumah and was the intellectual force behind a philosophy club founded by Nkrumah. He was also the club's leading philosophical theorist. In fact, he was Nkrumah's court philosopher and was brutalised by the new military rulers after Nkrumah was overthrown. Born in May 1934, he was almost 32 years old when Nkrumah was ousted and was vice chancellor of the University of Ghana during that time.

In the theoretical realm, Nkrumah's writings are a repetition of Marxist arguments and analysis so common among Marxists despite his attempt to formulate his own philosophy which would be distinctly his and reflective of African realities and relevant to African conditions. He was not an intellectual lightweight. But he lacked theoretical insights which would have enabled him to formulate and develop such a philosophy.

Even after years of refinement by its adherents – Kwame Ture being foremost among them - and their attempts to define it, Nkrumahism remains a nebulous concept. What is Nkrumahism? What is its essence? What are its underlying principles and essential elements *as an original philosophy and ideology*?

Even those who profess to be Nkrumahists have a hard time trying to define it and identify it as a distinct philosophy and ideology - except in general terms as a collection of Nkrumah's thoughts and ideas which collectively constitute a philosophy and an ideology called Nkrumahism for the establishment of a socioeconomic and political system of continental relevance.

Yet its underlying principles are no more than scientific socialism enunciated by Marx and Engels, repeated by Nkrumah. Without scientific socialism, there would be no Nkruhamism. Therefore, without Marx and Engels, and without Lenin, whose ideas inspired Nkrumah, there would be no Nkrumahism. And there would be no Nkrumah as a socialist thinker.

What would he be, as "an original thinker", without scientific socialism or if he had never even heard of it since that is what formed the foundation of "his own" philosophy?

Kofi Baako, one of Nkrumah's most trusted lieutenants who served as Leader of the House and Minister of State for Parliamentary Affairs and who also was the ruling party's ideologue – of the Convention People's Party (CPP) – put it "succinctly" when he defined Nkrumaism in an attempt to give it a distinct character in his article, "Nkrumaism – Its Theory and Practice," published in *The Party*, CPP Journal, Accra, 1961:

"I would define Nkrumaism as a nonatheistic socialist philosophy which seeks to apply the current socialist ideas to the solution(s) of our problems – be they domestic or international – by adapting these ideas to the realities of our everyday life. It is basically socialism adapted to suit the conditions and circumstances of Africa." – Kofi Baako, "Nkrumaism – Its Theory and Practice," in *The Party*, CPP Journal, Accra, Nos. 4 – 7, April, May, June and July, 1961; reprinted in Paul E. Sigmund, Jr., ed., *The Ideologies of the Developing Nations*, New York: Frederick A. Praeger, New York, 1963, p. 188; see also pp. 188 – 196. See also Kofi Baako, in Ebenezer Obiri Addo, *Kwame Nkrumah: A Case Study of Religion and Politics in Ghana*, Lanham, New York, Oxford: University Press of America, Inc., 1997, p. 159, when he made a futile attempt to define Nkrumaism as a distinct ideology in his address to Ghanaian envoys on 4 February 1962).

The last statement itself is a concession that the socialist ideas Kofi Baako wrote about did not come from

Africa.

A staunch Nkrumaist who worked with Nkrumah right from the beginning when they and their colleagues including Komla Gbedemah formed the Convention People's Party (CPP) in 1949, Kofi Baako was an avowed socialist who played a critical role in the formation of the CPP.

It was he who mobilised the youth to form a group which became the nucleus of the CPP, around which the party was formed. For that alone, he may even be credited for being the "founding father" of the Convention People's Party which led Ghana to independence and in pursuit of a socialist agenda; although it was Nkrumah's idea to form the party when he left the United Gold Coast Convention (UGCC) where he served as secretary-general; with Komla Gbedemah being acclaimed as the best CPP campaigner and mobiliser especially when Nkrumah was in prison.

The question is: Where did the socialist ideas Kofi Baako was talking about come from?

The socialism he was talking about came from Europe, ideas conceived by Karl Marx, unsuited to African conditions. That was in sharp contrast with Nyerere's socialism which was indigenous and suited to African conditions.

So, what made those ideas – from Europe – Nkrumaist? Why would they constitute Nkrumaism as a philosophy and as an ideology when they were not Nkrumah's original ideas?

Mere application of those ideas, even successfully, does not give legitimacy to the claim by Nkrumaists that it was a Nkrumaist ideology. It is the origin of ideas which gives an ideology a distinct character and identity. If they were Nyerere's, they would be Nyerereist. If they were Nkrumah's, they would be Nkrumaist. If they were Mao's, they would be Maoist. If they were Marx's, they would be Marxist – as they indeed were in this case.

Nkrumahism was a product of Marxism and Leninism, not of Nkrumah's own original ideas; hence Nkrumah's own admission that he was a Marxist and scientific socialist, unlike Nyerere who did not seek or get inspiration - and ideas - from outside Africa to formulate his own philosophy and ideology of African socialism known as *ujamaa*.

No other African leader attempted to do what Nyerere did in Tanzania – radically restructure society along socialist lines, including relocating large numbers of people in order to build ujamaa villages. Yet he did not – nor did anybody else in official circles – call this policy, Nyerereism, or a Nyerereist philosophy or ideology.

Also, there were other leaders who adopted Marxism-Leninism the way Nkrumah did. Yet they did not appropriate it and name it after themselves, except Nkrumah who called it Nkrumahism (or Nkrumaism).

Nkrumah's ideological compatriots, Ahmed Sekou Toure of Guinea and Modibo Keita of Mali tried to implement Marxism suited to local conditions. Yet they did not rename it after themselves. It was not called Toureism or a Toureist ideology and philosophy in Guinea; nor was it called Keitaism or Keitaist in Mali.

Mengistu Haile Mariam tried it in Ethiopia. He did not call it Mengistuism or Mariamism. Mathieu Kérékou tried it in Benin. Yet he did not call it Kerekouism. Samora Machel in Mozambique did not call the Marxism-Leninism he tried to implement – Samorist or Machelist. It was only Nkrumah who renamed the Marxism-Leninism he was trying to implement in Ghana – Nkrumaism (or Nkrumahism).

It is also true that socialism was the preferred ideology in many African countries soon after they won independence. Almost all the countries which tried to implement socialism adopted some form of Marxism or Leninism, except Tanzania under Nyerere. As Professor Mazrui stated in his book, *Towards a Pax Africana: A*

Study of Ideology and Ambition:

"No ideology commands respect so widely in Africa as the ideology of 'socialism' – though, as in Europe, it is socialism of different shades.

In Guinea and Mali a Marxist framework of reasoning is evident. In Ghana Leninism was wedded to notions of traditional collectivism. In Tanzania the concept of *Ujamaa*, derived from the sense of community of tribal life, is being radicalized into an assertion of modern socialism.

n Kenya there is a dilemma between establishing socialism and Africanizing the capitalism which already exists. In Nigeria, Senegal and Uganda some kind of allegiance is being paid to the ideal of social justice in situations with a multi-party background.

There are places, of course, where no school of socialism is propagated at all. But outside the Ivory Coast there is little defiant rejection of the idea of 'socialism' in former colonial Africa." – (Ali A. Mazrui, *Towards a Pax Africana: A Study of Ideology and Ambition*, London: Weidenfeld and Nicolson, 1967, p. 97. Cited by A. Mazrui, see also William H. Friedland and Carl G. Rosberg, Jr., eds., *African Socialism*, Stanford: Stanford University Press, 1964; Kenneth W. Grundy, "Marxism-Leninism: The Mali Approach,"*International Journal*, Vol. XVII, No. 3, Summer 1962; L. Gray Cowan, "Guinea," in Gwendolen M. Carter, ed., *African One-Party States*, Ithaca, New York: Cornell University Press, 1962; Kenneth W. Grundy, "Nkrumah's Theory of Underdevelopment: An Analysis of Recurrent Themes," *World Politics*, Vol. XV, No. 3, April 1963; Kenya Government Paper, *African Socialism and Its Application to Planning in Kenya*, 1965; *Africa Report*, Special issue on African Socialism, VIII, May 1963).

No other African leader tried to implement an

indigenous form of socialism the way Nyerere did, despite professions even by capitalist-oriented leaders such as Tom Mboya that African socialism was real and was the only form of socioeconomic system that was best for Africa. They did not go as far as Nyerere did, yet acknowledged the existence of socialism or socialist elements in traditional societies across the continent. As Mboya stated in *Transition*, Kampala, November 1963:

"I have not suggested that we have to go delving into the past seeking socialism. It is a continuing tradition among our people. Does the writer of the letter think that socialism had to be given a name before it became a reality? It is an attitude towards people practised in our societies and did not need to be codified into a scientific theory in order to find existence." – (Tom Mboya, *Transition*, Vol. 3, No. 11, November 1963, p. 6, cited by A.A. Mazrui, ibid., pp. 101, and 262).

Mboya was responding to a critic, C. N. Omondi (pen name), who wrote a letter to the editor, *Transition*, questioning the validity of the claim that socialism was indigenous to Africa. Omondi's letter was first published in *Kenya Weekly*, 2 August 1963.

In spite of Mboya's spirited defence of the existence of socialism in traditional societies across Africa, there is no question that socialism, in any form, was never practised in his home country, Kenya, as official or unofficial policy even when he was minister of economic planning. Among all African leaders, it was Nyerere who became the most articulate exponent and theorist of African socialism and its most consistent practitioner at the national level.

Nyerere said people in traditional societies across Africa lived on the basis of socialist values and principles, yet they had never even heard of Karl Marx. He elevated that to the national level and said we can build modern nations on that basis. Nkrumah said it had to be done on the basis of scientific socialism - hence Marxism; even if modified to suit African conditions, it was still an alien ideology imported from Europe whose relevance to Africa was questionable even though it inspired Nkrumah. That was the basis for Nkrumahism, also known as Nkrumaism and its exponents as Nkrumaists or Nkrumahists.

Marxism itself is now a discredited ideology, refuted by historical experience, as has been demonstrated by the collapse of communism around the world. Yet Nkrumahism continues to seek sustenance and validity from Marxism.

Nyerere gave an appropriate response to the disciples of Karl Marx and proponents of scientific socialism in the African context when he said Karl Marx was not an infallible divinity.

He said Africans don't need to be taught socialism by Karl Marx or by any other scientific socialists - it already existed in traditional societies across the continent. He went on to explain that it makes no sense to try to build our nations based on what Karl Marx wrote more than 100 years ago and on his analysis of conditions which prevailed in Europe, not in Africa, during his time when we can think for ourselves and find solutions to our problems based on our own analysis of the conditions which exist in our societies today. Nkrumaists say they already have answers - provided by Karl Marx more than 100 years ago.

Nkrumahism as a philosophy and as an ideology can *not* stand on its own as a product of an original thinker – there is nothing original about it. And it has failed to stand the test of time, unlike Marxism and Leninism. It has been shunted into oblivion. It is moribund at best. It may be in the political lexicon of Nkrumahists and a number of other militant or radical Pan-Africanists but hardly as a distinct ideology that is original and uniquely African like *ujamaa* expounded by Nyerere. Nkrumah himself was not even sure how to proceed in his quest for a doctrine that would define and underlie his political thought that would be distinctly his. As Colin Legum stated in his chapter,"Socialism in Ghana: A Political Interpretation," in *African Socialism*:

"(There were) growing divergences between *The Spark* and Nkrumah, especially during 1963 and the opening months of 1964, (which) have baffled outsiders. But it now seems clear that Nkrumah was deeply engaged in the search for a doctrine of socialism that would be of general application to Africa. His need was to reconcile his own socialist ideas with Pan-Africanism through a philosophy that would establish his position as a messianic leader on the continent.

He wished to do for Africa what Marx and Lenin had done for Europe and Mao Tse-tung for China. While willing to learn from them, he was unwilling to accept their philosophies. He therefore established his own Philosophy Club, with Professor Willie Abraham, a Ghanaian Fellow of All Souls, Oxford, as the main theoretician.

These philosophers, though sympathetic to Marxism, believed that neither the 'scientific socialists' nor the Western philosophers had supplied a doctrine that reflected the needs of Africa: these could come only from an understanding of African society.

Such an approach was not wholly acceptable to *The Spark* Marxists. While they were willing to cloak their 'scientific socialism' in *kente* cloth, they were opposed to thoroughgoing revisionism. They approached Africa entirely through Marxist eyes; the philosophers preferred to approach Marx through African eyes." – (Colin Legum, "Socialism in Ghana: A Political Interpretation," in William H. Friedland and Carl G. Rosberg, eds., *African Socialism*, Stanford, California, USA: Stanford University Press, 1964, p. 155).

Nkrumah himself approached Africa through Marxist eyes although in an attempt to adapt Marxism to African conditions. But the ideology was still Marxist and therefore not Nkrumah's or African. He himself said he was a Marxist even back then and maintained the same position throughout his life. He was *not* an African socialist like Nyerere whose socialist ideas were derived from the African traditional way of life based on the extended family and communal living, not from Marxist interpretations of the dynamics of society across the spectrum.

As a form of scientific socialism, Nkrumahism is irrelevant today, unlike Nyerere's African socialism since socialist elements still exist in traditional societies across the continent. The people in those societies continue to cherish, foster, and implement socialist values as they always have throughout our history, especially before the advent of colonial rule.

But Nkrumahism may have legitimacy in the political arena on the basis of three factors associated with Nkrumah: his quest for immediate continental unification, although it was and remains an unattainable ideal; formation of an African high command, first proposed by Nkrumah and which was a more realistic goal; and the concept of neocolonialism, advanced by Nkrumah and validated by experience; although the phenomenon itself – neocolonialism – had already been discerned by Nyerere as well who, in a speech in Dar es Salaam about three months before Tanganyika's independence in 1961, warned of the Second Scramble for Africa which would take place after African countries emerged from colonial rule.

In fact, Nyerere used the term "neo-imperialism" in June 1960 to describe the same phenomenon Nkrumah did when he coined the term "neocolonialism" later.

Therefore, what was new was *not* the phenomenon but only the term "neocolonialism" Nkrumah coined to describe it. He probably coined it in 1963, when it was first used, or just before then, while Nyerere used the term "neo-imperialism" three years before then to describe the *same* phenomenon. As Nyerere stated in June 1960:

"In the struggle against colonialism the fundamental unity of the people of Africa is evident and is deeply felt. It is, however, a unity forged in diversity in a battle against an outside Government.

If the triumph in this battle is to be followed by an equal triumph against the forces of neo-imperialism and also against poverty, ignorance and disease, then this unity must be strengthened and maintained." – (Julius K. Nyerere, "Freedom and Unity,"*Transition, Volume 0, Issue 14, 1964*, Kampala, Uganda, pp. 40 – 45. This was a republication of what he wrote earlier in June 1960 before he led Tanganyika to independence the following year. For an analysis of cooperation among the three East African countries of Kenya, Uganda and Tanganyika, see also Donald Rothschild, *Politics of Integration: An East African Documentary*, Nairobi, Kenya: East African Publishing House, 1968).

As a theoretician, Nkrumah did not attain stature comparable to Karl Marx, Lenin and Mao in the global arena as he hoped he would, especially as Africa's "messianic figure." But he was in the same league with Nyerere as one of the world's historical giants. As Professor Mazrui stated in his eulogy of Nyerere: "He was one of the giants of the 20th century....He did bestride this narrow world like an African colossus." So did Nkrumah, but not as an original thinker like Nyerere.

Also, Nkrumah did not really write his most controversial book, *Neo-Colonialism: The Last Stage of Imperialism*(published in October 1965 to coincide with the OAU Accra summit), which infuriated American leaders and was one of the reasons they decided to overthrow him. The book, which was an extension of Lenin's *Imperialism: The Highest Stage of Capitalism*, was actually written by other people although in collaboration with Nkrumah. They included Shirley Graham Du Bois, an African American who was the widow of Dr. W.E. B. Du Bois; Dorothy Pizer, a white British woman who was the partner of George Padmore, Nkrumah's adviser on African affairs; and Hodee Edwards, a white American woman who was a renowned Marxist and whose husband was an African American.

Hodee Edwards also worked for the Ghanaian government to provide an intellectual rationale for scientific socialism and refute the validity of African socialism, a position articulated by Abdulrahman Mohamed Babu in the Tanzanian context – outside officialdom.

They all lived in Accra during that period and worked closely with Nkrumah. But Nkrumah's contribution to the book was minimal, in terms of writing, besides supporting the work's central thesis which was elaborated by Hodee Edwards. She played the biggest role in writing the book. Details on the exploitation of Africa by the United States, especially by American corporations, and other facts about the imperial nature of the world's most powerful country came from her; and partly from other pro-Nkrumah Americans such as Shirley Du Bois who was not even allowed to visit the United States to see her friends and relatives soon after Nkrumah was overthrown. She was denied a visa by the American embassy in Accra.

She and her husband moved to Ghana in 1961. They became citizens in 1963 shortly before Dr. W.E.B. Du Bois died. They moved to Ghana at the invitation of Nkrumah. Nkrumah also asked Dr. W.E.B. Du Bois to be the leader of a team that was working on a major project about Africa and the African diaspora: compiling the *Encyclopedia Africana* about the Pan-African world.

Dr. Du Bois is considered by many people in the Pan-

African world to be the father of Pan-Africanism because of the role he played in organising Pan-African conferences and championing the cause of African independence. Nkrumah and Nnamdi Azikiwe were among the people he inspired when they were students in the United States. He died in Accra in August 1963 and was buried there. He was 95 years old.

Had he lived longer, it is possible he could have moved to Tanzania and become a Tanzanian with his wife after Nkrumah was overthrown and replaced by a regime that was hostile to them because of their support for him. Tanzania was held in high esteem by many people in the Pan-African world and elsewhere because of Nyerere's leadership but also incurred the wrath of the imperial powers because of its anti-imperialist stance.

The refusal by the American authorities to allow Shirley Du Bois to go to the United States showed their hostility towards those who supported Nkrumah. Also, the decision by the Du Boises to renounce their American citizenship was not well-received by the American leaders; it was considered to be an insult to them and their great country.

The problems Shirley Du Bois faced when she tried to get a visa to visit the land of her birth, where she had lived her entire life before moving to Ghana, also showed the extent to which the United States was willing to go to punish Nkrumah's allies and supporters.

She even became a citizen of Tanzania and travelled on a Tanzanian passport. But that did not help her enter the United States. The United States did not have very good relations with Tanzania. Also Nyerere, like Sekou Toure, was known to be a strong supporter of Nkrumah. He even offered him asylum but Nkrumah decided to go to Guinea. Nyerere also strongly condemned the coup against Nkrumah when he spoke at a press conference in Dar es Salaam about Nkrumah's ouster.

Nyerere and Nkrumah were also greatly admired by

many black Americans (African Americans) and had basically the same attitude towards the United States as an imperial power which wanted to dominate Africa. About 10 years after Nkrumah was overthrown, Shirley Du Bois, who greatly admired Nyerere as much as she did Nkrumah, even wrote a book about Nyerere, *Julius K. Nyerere: Teacher of Africa*, published in 1975. As Professor Gerald Horne states in his book, *Race Woman: The Lives of Shirley Graham Du Bois*, about the problems Mrs. Du Bois had with the American authorities:

"Weeks before the coup (against Nkrumah and which was engineered by the United States), she applied for a thirty-day visa to visit the United States, noting that she had not been to the 'land of my birth' since October 1961, but now she wanted to 'visit my brothers in California, friends in the New York area,' and others...Her visa was denied....

In 1970 she and David (her son) had gone to the Ghanaian embassy in Cairo to renew her passport; unfortunately, they 'were received with extreme discourtesy.' By this point Kwame Nkrumah, who initially had been seen as a virtual co-leader of Guinea with Sekou Toure, was old news; she concluded with sadness that 'it would appear' that Nkrumah 'no longer has any influence where he is,' so a Guinean passport seemed out of the question.

Eventually she was to obtain a Tanzanian passport, but this nation did not have ideal relations with Washington either.

Ultimately she was to receive a visa to return to the United States, but not without considerable lobbying and protest. She returned to a land that in some ways seemed light years away from the nation she had departed only a few years earlier....U.S. authorities were worried that 'a refusal of a visa to Mrs. Du Bois might lead to adverse reaction in certain African nations as well as in the U.S.'" -

(Gerald Horne, R*ace Woman: The Lives of Shirley Graham Du Bois*, New York: New York University Press, 2000, pp. 212, and 252 - 253).

Shirley Graham Du Bois died in Beijing, China, on 27 March 1977, as a Tanzanian. She was was accorded a state funeral:

"It was Saturday of April 1977 in Beijing, China. The auditorium at the Paposhan Cemetery for Revolutionaries was full. The vice premier, Chen Yung-kuei, and the widow of former premier Zhou Enlai were among the dignitaries present. The Communist Party chairman, Hua Kuo-feng, sent a wreath to this 'memorial meeting,' as did the embassies of Tanzania, Ghana, and Zambia.

These leaders and ordinary citizens had come to mourn the passing of a woman, born an African American, who died in China as a citizen of Tanzania.

Shirley Graham Du Bois—the name that most knew her by—was eighty years old and had come to the Chinese capital for medical treatment....

China was also quite close to Graham Du Bois's eventual adopted home, Tanzania; according to one analyst, Dar es Salaam by the early 1970s 'had probably developed more extensive ties with that country than with any other non-African state'....

Many of her duties as an activist and a writer concerned her 'motherland,' Africa. At a time when many African Americans shunned the continent in embarrassment because of its underdevelopment, she was presenting an alternative vision....

She wrote biographies of leading African personalities, worked at the shoulder of Nkrumah when he was seeking to build a 'United States of Africa,' and became a citizen of Ghana, then Tanzania....

(She eventually settled in Dar es salaam, Tanzania, although) Nkrumah advised her, recommending that she stay away from Tanzania in her search for a post-coup home, for 'East Africa at the moment is filled up with American agents—CIA and so forth. I don't trust these 'guys'....

She encountered many...exiles in Dar es Salaam, a frequent port of call for her after 1966 (the year she left Ghana soon after Nkrumah was overthrown). She became quite friendly with the nation's leader, Julius Nyerere, whom she addressed as 'my dear Mwalimu' or teacher.....When she traveled to the southeast African republic, she would meet with him 'not only in his office, but with the family in his home.' Her affection for the Tanzanian leader was revealed in her hagiographic biography of him." - (Ibid., pp. 25, 27, 29, 217, and 251).

Her support for Nkrumah had cost her dearly. But Nkrumah remained a respected figure in the African-American community; his stature as a Pan-Africanist icon enhanced by the belief that it was the United States which was behind the military coup against him; a coup that was partly attributed to Nkrumah's bitter criticism of the United States in his book, *Neo-Colonialism: The Last Stage of Imperialism.* As Robert Smith, a former American ambassador to Ghana, stated in an interview:

"Nkrumah dropped the straw that broke the camel's back, so to speak, in that he published a new book called *Neo-Colonialism* (*The Last State of Imperialism*)...which was simply outrageous. It accused the United States of every sin imaginable to man. We were blamed for everything in the world.

The book was so bad that I remember the then Assistant Secretary (of state for African affairs), G. Mennen Williams, called me up and gave me that book and said, 'Bob, I know this is bad. I don't know how bad. I want you to take it home tonight and read it. You're not going to get any sleep and I apologize for that, but on my desk, by eight o'clock tomorrow morning, I've got to have a written summary of this because I have called the Ghanaian ambassador in at ten o'clock tomorrow morning. We're going to protest this book.'

There had already been advance publicity so we knew it was bad, but we hadn't had our hands on a copy. And it was everything we feared it would be. It was awful.

And the next morning – of course, he had me in on this meeting as the note taker – a lovely, old man, Michael Ribiero, was the Ghanaian ambassador. Hated Nkrumah privately, but was a good soldier trying to put the best face on this, a career officer in their foreign service and very respected here and in Ghana.

Governor Williams, of course, was a relatively mild-mannered man. I had never heard Soapy Williams raise his voice until that conversation. Neither have I ever heard an ambassador get a tongue lashing like Ribiero got from Assistant Secretary Williams that morning.

He, unfortunately, tried a couple times to interrupt the governor when he was making a point. He had my notes in front of him. And at one point, when Ribiero interrupted him, he said, 'Just a minute, Mr. Ambassador, don't interrupt me. I'm not through.'

And he continued to go on.

He was raising his voice. He was shaking his finger in the ambassador's face. And it was a very painful, hour-long interview. To put it mildly, he protested vigorously the contents and publication of this book.

I think the publication of that book might also have contributed in a material way to his overthrow shortly thereafter." - (Ambassador Robert P. Smith, interviewed by Charles Stuart Kennedy, 28 February 1989, *The Association for Diplomatic Studies and Training, Foreign Affairs Oral History Project*, pp. 12 – 15).

The book was Marxist in terms of analysis and Leninist in ideological orientation with regard to the imperialist nature of capitalism as a predatory system and imperialism being the highest stage of capitalism, thus in accord with Nkrumah's thinking although it was ghost-written. But it was Nkrumah who propounded the work's central thesis. Also, it was he who coined the term "neo-colonialism" to describe the insidious nature of the machinations of the imperial powers to dominate and control former colonies after they attained sovereign status.

The central thesis of *Neo-Colonialism: The Last Stage of Imperialism* also reflected Nkrumah's profound mistrust – perhaps even hatred – of the United States as an imperial power ruthlessly exploiting Africa and wreaking havoc across the continent; a belief that was reinforced by what happened during the Congo crisis, including Lumumba's assassination, for which the United States was largely responsible.

He gave a passionate speech at the United Nations, accusing imperial - Western - powers of interfering in African affairs in an attempt to control the destiny of the continent, and even wrote a book, *Challenge of the Congo: A Case Study of Foreign Pressures in an Independent State*, to explain what happened in "the bleeding heart of Africa" during that period and what needed to be done for African countries to be genuinely independent.

His memory is invoked even today whenever there is a crisis in Africa attributed to disunity among Africans and whenever there is foreign intervention in continental affairs to serve the interests of external forces; the lesson being: had African leaders agreed to unite their countries under one government as Nkrumah advocated, none of this would be happening. And although many of his arguments lacked originality, there is no question that he was very good at using Marxist arguments in different analytical contexts to justify his position.

He was also probably the most daring African leader in

the continent's post-colonial history, demonstrated by his passionate call for immediate continental unification under one government and for the invasion of Rhodesia by Ghanaian troops to overthrow the white minority regime; goals most of his colleagues thought were unrealistic and even reckless as well as premature considering the fact that other African leaders were not ready to relinquish power for the sake of continental unity, and the invasion of Rhodesia by Ghanaian forces would have been a logistical nightmare without the direct involvement of Tanzania and Zambia.

May be he thought by using the Ghanaian army to try and free Rhodesia, other African countries would have been forced to send troops to the combat zone had Nyerere and Kaunda supported his mission to use Tanzania and Zambia as operational and rear bases; an unlikely prospect during that time. Also, apartheid South Africa would have entered the war to support the white minority regime in Rhodesia. But that was Nkrumah, the visionary.

Yet, some of his lofty ideals did not correspond to reality; his quest for immediate continental unification in the sixties being the most unrealistic.

He ignored the formidable opposition he faced from other African leaders who did not want to unite their countries under one government; most of them didn't. They were not even interested in forming an exploratory committee which could have helped chart the course towards unification. That is why Nyerere told Nkrumah "We are not going to have an African Napoleon" who is going to force other African leaders to unite their countries now – or even in the future - if they were not ready or if they did not want to do so. A regional approach towards unity – for example, by forming economic blocs even before considering regional federation under one government - seemed to be more acceptable to some of them. As Nyerere stated in his speech in Accra on the 40th anniversary of Ghana's independence in March 1997:

"Prior to independence of Tanganyika, I had been advocating that East African countries should federate and then achieve independence as a single political unit. I had said publicly that I was willing to delay Tanganyika's independence in order to enable all three-mainland countries to achieve their independence together as a single federated state.

I made the suggestion because of my fear, proved correct by later events, that it would be very difficult to unite our countries if we let them achieve independence separately.

Once you multiply national anthems, national flags and national passports, seats at the United Nations, and individuals entitled to 21-gun salute, not to speak of a host of ministers, prime ministers, and envoys, you will have a whole army of powerful people with vested interests in keeping Africa balkanized. That was what Nkrumah encountered in 1965.

After the failure to establish the union government at the Accra summit of 1965, I heard one head of state express with relief that he was happy to be returning home to his country still head of state. To this day I cannot tell whether he was serious or joking. But he may well have been serious, because Kwame Nkrumah was very serious and the fear of a number of us to lose our precious status was quite palpable.

But I never believed that the 1965 Accra summit would have established a union government for Africa. When I say that we failed, that is not what I mean, for that clearly was an unrealistic objective for a single summit. What I mean is that we did not even discuss a mechanism for pursuing the objective of a politically united Africa. We had a Liberation Committee already. We should have at least had a Unity Committee or undertaken to establish one. We did not. And after Kwame Nkrumah was removed from the African political scene nobody took up the challenge again."

One of Nyerere's critics and admirers, Professor Ali Mazrui, stated in some of his lectures and writings that it was Nyerere, not Nkrumah, who was vindicated by history on how African countries should pursue the goal of continental unity.

A few years before he died, Professor Mazrui also said "Nkrumah: The Leninist Czar" was the most controversial - and most influential - article he ever wrote that was still being debated in academic circles and elsewhere decades later.

He was strongly criticised by some of Nkrumah's supporters and admirers who denounced him as "an imperialist agent." Nkrumah himself, who read the article when he was in exile in Conakry, Guinea, said it was written by a black neo-colonial intellectual. The two first met in 1961 when Mazrui was a student at Columbia University in New York where he was studying for his master's degree in political science and got the chance to ask Nkrumah a question at a meeting of African students which the Ghanaian leader also addressed. Nkrumah spoke at Columbia during his visit to New York where he also addressed the United Nations. He also visited Harlem where he once lived when he was a student in the United States.

Mazrui angered even more Ghanaians when, in a lecture at the University of Ghana and elsewhere in Accra in the 2000s, and in some of his writings, he stated: "Nkrumah was a great African, but not a great Ghanaian." According to Mazrui himself:

"Most Ghanaian intellectuals seem aware of my notorious article of 1966 titled, 'Nkrumah: The Leninist Czar.' The article has two controversial arguments. Firstly, while Nkrumah was ideologically a Leninist, he was in style of governance a Czar when he was in power. An even more explosive paradox of mine was that Nkrumah was a great African, but not a great Ghanaian.

In 2007, as during my earlier visits to Ghana, I was repeatedly questioned about those two assertions. Militant Nkrumahists and members of his old party (the C.P.P.) were outraged by my views and argued back vehemently both at my lectures and during radio phone-in interviews.

At another lecture I gave at the W.E.B. Du Bois Pan-African Cultural Centre in Accra the debate about Nkrumah exploded into a walkout by a couple of enraged Nkrumahists

But we should remember that Ghana continues to be deeply divided about Kwame Nkrumah, their most illustrious post-colonial son and their founder president. There are at least as many Ghanaians who agree with my conclusions about Nkrumah as disagree." - (Ali A. Mazrui, *Mazrui Newsletter No. 32*, Spring 2008, p. 13).

It is a highly contentious subject, especially when one takes into account the fact that it was Nkrumah who laid the foundation for modern Ghana – the infrastructure, industrialisation, and so on. Yet the argument persists that "he was not a great Ghanaian" because he pursued his Pan-African goals at the expense of Ghana, including liberation and continental unification under one socialist government, probably a Marxist one since he was a Marxist himself; a position that was somewhat different from Nyerere's in terms of continental unity. As Nyerere stated in an interview with Ikaweba Bunting of the *New Internationalist*:

"For me liberation and unity were the most important things. I have always said that I was African first and socialist second. I would rather see a free and united Africa before a fragmented socialist Africa. I did not preach socialism. I made this distinction deliberately so as not to divide the country.

The majority in the anti-colonial struggle were nationalist. There was a minority who argued that class was the central issue, that white workers were exploited as black workers by capitalism. They wanted to approach liberation in purely Marxist terms. However, in South Africa white workers oppressed black workers. It was more than class and I saw that....Even now for me freedom and unity are paramount." - (Mwalimu Julius K. Nyerere, in an interview with Ikaweba Bunting, *New Internationalist*, Oxford, UK, January-February 1999).

Unlike Nyerere, Nkrumah was a Marxist throughout his political career. In fact, he embraced Marxism in the early forties when he was a student in the United States. Years later, he even wrote a book, *Class Struggle in Africa*, based on Marxist analysis.

Colin Legum, in his review of Nkrumah's first book, *Towards Colonial Freedom*, also clearly stated that Nkrumah's political thought – at least a substantial part of it on social, political and economic theory - was a product of Marxism and Leninism. As he stated:

"*Towards Colonial Freedom* is a restatement of imperialism as propounded by Lenin. Dr. Nkrumah has, of course, never concealed his own Marxist beliefs." - (Colin Legum, *The Journal of Modern African Studies, Vol. 1, Issue 01*, March 1963, pp. 125 – 126).

Nkrumah's book, whose whole title was *Towards Colonial Freedom: Africa in the Struggle Against World Imperialism*, was first published in London in October 1947 when Nkrumah was not yet actively involved in politics in his home country, the Gold Coast. He returned to the Gold Coast – from the UK – on a ship with his friend and classmate at Lincoln University, Ako Adjei, in November 1947. Ako Adjei himself played a major role in the struggle for Ghana's independence - he was one of The

Big Six who led the anti-colonial struggle as members of the United Gold Coast Convention (UGCC) - but later fell out with Nkrumah and was imprisoned by him.

Besides Lenin, Nkrumah's book (*Towards Colonial Freedom*) and his analysis of imperialism was also based on the work of another prominent Marxist, Rosa Luxemburg.

Nkrumah himself, in acknowledgement of his Marxist beliefs, embraced scientific socialism – developed by Marx and Engels – as the only form of true socialism, thus differing with Nyerere who espoused African socialism. As Ama Biney states in her book, *The Political and Social Thought of Kwame Nkrumah*:

"During the four years Nkrumah spent in Conakry, through his letters to various individuals, his thinking on many social, political, and economic issues can be delienated.

When his research assistant, June Milne, expressed an interest in writing a book on Nkrumaism, Nkrumah wrote, 'The most tantalising part of it will be my Marxist or socialist ideology. You know I am a Marxist and scientific socialist. But I don't consider myself in this particular sense a Leninist. Leninism is an application of Marxism to the Russian milieu. But the Russian milieu is not the same as the African milieu. And here the question of communism comes in – whether I am a communist or not. I am a scientific socialist and a Marxist and if that is tantamount to being a communist then I am. But not a communist of the Marxist-Leninist type.'

Here Nkrumah openly acknowledged his Marxist beliefs. He considered Marxism to be a nondogmatic tool applied to different social and economic conditions. However, he did not define what type of communist he was and, therefore, ambiguity remains as to his definition. In short, Nkrumah was undoctrinaire in his application of Marxist analysis to African realities." – (Ama Biney, *The*

Political and Social Thought of Kwame Nkrumah, New York: Palgrave Macmillan, 2011, pp. 162 – 163).

Sharply contrasted with that is Nyerere's position on Marxism-Leninism and scientific socialism. His position is rooted in indigenous thought, instead of embracing imported -isms such as Marxism to find solutions to African problems. He was not a doctrinaire socialist like those who espoused Marxist dogma. As he stated in his book, *Freedom and Socialism*:

"There is no theology of socialism. There is, however, an apparent tendency among certain socialists to try and establish a new religion – a religion of socialism itself. This is usually called 'scientific socialism' and the works of Marx and Lenin are regarded as the holy writ in the light of which all other thoughts and actions have to be judged....Its proponents are often most anxious to decry religion as the 'opium of the people,' and they present their beliefs as 'science.' Yet they talk and act in the same manner as the most rigid of theologians.

We find them condemning one another's actions because they do not accord with what the priests of 'scientific socialism' have decided is the true meaning, in modern terms, of books written more than 100 years ago.

Indeed we are fast getting to the stage where quarrels between different Christian sects about the precise meaning of the Bible fade into insignificance when compared with the quarrels of those who claim to be the true interpreters of Marxism-Leninism!

This attempt to create a new religion out of socialism is absurd. It is not scientific, and it is almost certainly not Marxist – for however combatant and quarrelsome a socialist Marx was, he never claimed to be an infallible divinity! Marx was a great thinker. He gave a brilliant analysis of the industrial capitalist society in which he lived; he diagnosed its ills and advocated certain remedies which he believed would lead to the development of a healthy society. But he was not God.

The years have proved him wrong in certain respects just as they have proved him right in others. Marx did not write revealed truth; his books are the result of hard thinking and hard work, not a revelation from God. It is therefore unscientific to appeal to his writings as Christians appeal to the Bible, or Muslims to the Koran.

The works of Marx and Lenin are useful to a socialist because these men thought about the objective conditions of their time and tried to work out the actions necessary to achieve certain ends. We can learn from their methods of analysis, and from their ideas. But the same is true of many other thinkers of the past.

It is no part of the job of a socialist in 1968 to worry about whether or not his actions or proposals are in accordance with what Marx or Lenin wrote, and it is a waste of time and energy to spend hours – if not months and years – trying to prove that what you have decided is objectively necessary is really in accordance with their teachings.

The task of a socialist is to think out for himself the best way of achieving desired ends under the conditions which exist now. It is his job to think how to organize society, how to solve a particular problem, or how to effect certain changes, in a manner which will emphasize the importance of man and the equality of man.

It is especially important that we in Africa should understand this. We are groping our way forward towards socialism, and we are in danger of being bemused by this new theology, and therefore of trying to solve our problems according to what the priests of Marxism say is what Marx said or meant. If we do this we shall fail.

Africa's conditions are very different from those of the Europe in which Marx and Lenin wrote and worked. To talk as if these thinkers provided all the answers to our problems, or as if Marx invented socialism, is to reject both the humanity of Africa and the universality of socialism. Marx did contribute a great deal to socialist thought. But socialism did not begin with him, nor can it end in constant reinterpretation of his writings.

Speaking generally, and despite the existence of a few feudalistic communities, traditional Tanzanian society had many socialist characteristics. The people did not call themselves socialists, and they were not socialists by deliberate design. But all the people were workers, there was no living off the sweat of others. There was no very great difference in the amount of goods available to the different members of the society. All these are socialist characteristics.

Despite the low level of material progress, traditional African society was in practice organized on a basis which was in accordance with socialist principles.

These conditions still prevail over large areas of Tanzania – and indeed in many other parts of Africa. Even in our urban areas, the social expectation of sharing what you have with your kinsfolk is still very strong – and causes great problems for individuals! These things have nothing to do with Marx; the people have never heard of him. Yet they provide a basis on which modern socialism can be built. To reject this base is to accept the idea that Africa has nothing to contribute to the march of mankind; it is to argue that the only way progress can be achieved in Africa is if we reject our own past and impose on ourselves the doctrines of some other society.

Nor would it be very scientific to reject Africa's past when trying to build socialism in Africa. For, scientific socialism means finding out all the facts in a particular situation, regardless of whether you like them or not, or whether they fit in with preconceived ideas. It means analysing these facts, and then working out solutions to the problems you are concerned with in the light of these facts, and of the objectives you are trying to achieve.

This is what Marx did in Europe in the middle of the

nineteenth century; if he had lived in Sukumaland, Masailand, or Ruvuma, he would have written a different book than *Das Kapital*, but he could have been just as scientific and just as socialist. For if 'scientific socialism' means anything, it can only mean that the objectives are socialist and you apply scientific methods of study in working out the appropriate policies.

If the phrase does not mean that, then it is simply a trap to ensnare the unwary into a denunciation of their own nature therefore into a new form of oppression. For a scientist works to discover truth. He does not claim to know it, nor is he seeking to discover truth as revealed — which is the job of the theologian. A scientist works on the basis of the knowledge which has been accumulated empirically, and which is held to be true until new experience demonstrates otherwise, or demonstrates a superior truth which takes precedence in particular situations.

A really scientific socialist would therefore start his analysis of the problems of a particular society from the standpoint of that society. In Tanzania he would take the existence of some socialist values as part of his material for analysis; he would study the effect of the colonial era on these attitudes and on the systems of social organization; he would take account of the world situation as it affects Tanzania. After doing all that he would try to work out policies appropriate for the growth of a modern socialist state. And he could well finish up with the Arusha Declaration and the policies of ujamaa!

A scientific socialist could do all this with or without a knowledge and understanding of Marx and Lenin — or for that matter Saint-Simon, Owen or Laski. Knowledge of the work and thinking of these and other people may help a socialist to know what to look for and how to evaluate the things he sees; but it could also mislead him if he is not careful.

Equally, a knowledge of history may help him to learn

from the experience of others; a knowledge of economics will help him to understand some of the forces at work in the society. But if he tries to use any of these disciplines and philosophies as a gospel according to which he must work out solutions he will go wrong. There is no substitute for his own hard work and hard thinking." – (Julius K. Nyerere, *Freedom and Socialism: A Selection from Writings and Speeches 1965 – 1967*, Dar es Salaam: Oxford University Press, 1968, pp. 14 – 17).

C.L.R. James hailed the Arusha Declaration, which Nyerere wrote in an attempt to transform Tanzania into a socialist society, as "the highest stage of resistance ever reached by revolting Blacks."

When Nyerere himself was asked in an interview in December 1998, "Does the Arusha Declaration still stand up today?", he said in response:

"I still travel around with it. I read it over and over to see what I would change. Maybe I would improve on the Kiswahili that was used but the Declaration is still valid: I would not change a thing.

Tanzania had been independent for a short time before we began to see a growing gap between the haves and the have-nots in our country. A privileged group was emerging from the political leaders and bureaucrats who had been poor under colonial rule but were now beginning to use their positions in the Party and the Government to enrich themselves.

This kind of development would alienate the leadership from the people. So we articulated a new national objective: we stressed that development is about all our people and not just a small and privileged minority.

The Arusha Declaration was what made Tanzania distinctly Tanzania. We stated what we stood for, we laid down a code of conduct for our leaders and we made an effort to achieve our goals." - (Nyerere, and C.L.R. James,

New Internationalist, ibid.)

C.L.R. James had this to say about Nyerere and Tanzania under Mwalimu's leadership:

"The opportunity arrived for me to go to Tanzania. I spent eight or ten days there. I talked to a lot of people, I travelled about a lot, I had an interview with Nyerere and I am satisfied that what they are doing is something entirely new, not only for Africa but in the political systems of the world that we have known. Nothing like it has appeared since Lenin died in 1924....

Nyerere has understood what has been the cause of the collapse of the other African states and knew that if he didn't put blocks in the road of that he was going to go the same way. This is the reason why this has taken place....Nyerere...has introduced policies which strike at all the weaknesses of the colonial African state, all the weaknesses that have remained....

Nyerere and TANU are beginning to find out, to restore, the African family, and to understand that this special group of people who are educated, who become bureaucrats, they are the ones who must be separated, they must be educated so as to become part of the population and bring the knowledge that they have as part of the population which the majority of the people constitute....Nothing like that has ever taken place in Africa anywhere.

Nkrumah, it seemed at the beginning, hoped to do something of the kind, but he didn't make these drastic changes in the economic and social structure that Nyerere has made, and it is my belief, I have talked to Nyerere, that he did it because he realized that unless these fundamental changes were made and the old structures and the ideas that the British and the French had left behind, unless these were completely cleared out and the people given another perspective, the degeneration of the African state was bound to continue....

There is one of the most important features of political development in the world today, not only for the underdeveloped countries but, I am positive, I have examined it, the advanced countries, in their systems of education in particular, have a lot to learn from what is taking place in Tanzania." - (C.L.R. James, "Reflections on Pan-Africanism," ibid.)

Nkrumah did a lot for Ghana in the few years he was in power. But he did not do enough to radically transform Ghana into a socialist society the way Nyerere did in Tanzania.

Still, like Nyerere, Nkrumah left a legacy, especially with regard to the continent's destiny, that is still being debated: Where would Africa be today had the continent united under one government in 1963 or soon thereafter, as he strongly advocated? Was it a realistic goal? Or was a regional approach to continental unification a more viable option? Would socialism have been adopted on a continental scale had African countries succeeded in uniting under one government? As Nyerere stated:

"Kwame Nkrumah and I were committed to the idea of unity. African leaders and heads of state did not take Kwame seriously. However, I did. I did not believe in these small little nations. Still today I do not believe in them. I tell our people to look at the European Union, at these people who ruled us who are now uniting.

Kwame and I met in 1963 and discussed African Unity. We differed on how to achieve a United States of Africa. But we both agreed on a United States of Africa as necessary. Kwame went to Lincoln University, a black college in the US. He perceived things from the perspective of US history, where 13 colonies that revolted against the British formed a union. That is what he thought the OAU (Organisation of African Unity) should do.

I tried to get East Africa to unite before independence.

When we failed in this way, I was wary about Kwame's continental approach. We corresponded profusely on this. Kwame said my idea of 'regionalization' was only balkanization on a larger scale. Later, African historians will have to study our correspondence on this issue of uniting Africa." - (Nyerere, *New Internationalist*, ibid.)

Yet Nkrumah himself formed a regional federation – of Ghana, Guinea and Mali (with Guinea in 1958, and Mali joining in 1961) – but it collapsed; in fact, it was more symbolic than functional.

It was only after he failed in his attempt to form a functional union of the three West African countries that he started opposing regional federations, claiming they were no more than balkanisation of the continent on a grand scale. Even when he was in London for two and a half years, after he left the United States in 1945, he worked with other West Africans in the UK in an attempt to form a West African federation in the future.

He did not see all that as balkanisation of Africa on a larger scale – until Nyerere tried to form a federation in East Africa and seemed to be succeeding. Nkrumah did not like that. He wanted to be the first, but failed in his regional attempt to form a federation in West Africa.

He was resolutely opposed to formation of an East African federation and did everything he could to sabotage it. This infuriated Nyerere who, in pointed reference to Nkrumah, publicly stated at a press conference in Nairobi in June 1963 after the three East African leaders – Kenyatta, Obote and Nyerere himself – met to discuss forming a federation:

"We must reject some of the pretensions that have been made from outside East Africa. We have already heard the curious argument that the continued 'balkanisation' of East Africa will somehow help African unity.... These are attempts to rationalize absurdity." – (Julius Nyerere, quoted by Richard Cox, *Pan-Africanism in Practice: An*

East African Study, Oxford University Press, 1964, p. 77; A. Mazrui, *Towards a Pax Africana*, op. cit., p. 71).

Nkrumah's interference in East African affairs angered Nyerere so much that he even wrote Nkrumah about it:

"His meddling became so apparent that on 6th August, 1963, President Nyerere of Tanzania wrote him a very angry letter on this subject." – Donald S. Rothchild, *Politics of Integration: An East African Documentary*, Institute of Development Studies, University College of Nairobi; East African Publishing House, Nairobi, Kenya, 1968, p. 112).

Nkrumah's interference in East Africa to frustrate and neutralise Nyerere's attempt to form an East African federation was one of the biggest mistakes of his political career and demonstrated that he was determined to undermine other African leaders who did not agree with him. As Basil Davidson stated in his book, *Black Star: A View of the Life and Times of Kwame Nkrumah*:

"Some, like Julius Nyerere of Tanzania, chastised Nkrumah for his interference. East Africa, Nyerere believed, could best contribute to continental unity by moving first towards regional unity.
Although knowing little about East Africa, Nkrumah not only disagreed but actively interfered to obstruct the East African federation proposed by Nyerere.... It was one of Nkrumah's worst mistakes." – (Basil Davidson, *Black Star: A View of the Life and Times of Kwame Nkrumah*, Allen Lane, London, 1973, quoted by Geoffrey Mmari, "The Legacy of Nyerere," in Colin Legum and Geoffrey Mmari, eds., *Mwalimu: The Influence of Nyerere*, Africa World Press, Trenton, New Jersey, 1995, pp. 179 – 180).

Renowned Kenyan socio-political analyst, Philip

Ochieng, who once worked as a columnist of the *Daily News*, Dar es Salaam, Tanzania, in the early seventies, stated in his article,"Did Nkrumah Kill Off the First EA Community?," in *The East African*, Nairobi, 28 March 2009:

"According to the story that I kept hearing...from top-level academics...at the University of Dar es Salaam... known to enjoy direct links with Mwalimu's State House, it was because Dr Nkrumah wanted to be the father figure of all the regional initiatives, that he sabotaged the East African chapter...

Nkrumah himself sponsored a West African initiative similar to the proposed East African federation...composed of his Ghana, Ahmed Sekou Toure's Guinea and Modibo Keita's Mali....As long as he was the paramount leader of such an initiative, there was no problem.

In East Africa, Nyerere was also taking serious steps to restructure his society. Tanzania (under Nyerere), indeed, is the African country that has gone farthest in dismantling the political, economic and intellectual pillars of colonialism....

Nkrumah...wanted to be the dominant figure in every regional initiative. Like Joseph Stalin for all of the world's non-Maoist communist parties, Nkrumah wanted to be chief policy-maker and policy implementer for every one of the regional groupings. The probable idea was that, if all those regional groupings decided to unite into a single continental government, no individual would be in a position to vie with the Ghanaian leader to be its first president.

That was why Nkrumah could not trust Mwalimu Nyerere as the intellectual spirit behind the East African proposal. For, although they seemed like ideological comrades, the old Tanganyikan schoolteacher was completely independent-minded and would never have been prepared to act as Nkrumah's regional poodle.

With Nyerere thus dismissed and Mzee Kenyatta accused of having surrendered Kenya as a backyard of corporate Britain, the Ubungo intellectuals explained that, in Nkrumah's eyes, Obote now appeared as the only one not too committed one way or the other. That was why – according to the story – it was Obote that Nkrumah latched onto to frustrate all the plans to federate."

The role Uganda played under Obote to sabotage federation of the the East African countries may have been underestimated. It was not publicly known, although Nkrumah's interference was public knowledge, at least among a number of people in academia and in the political arena especially the political elite. As Professor Azaria Mbughuni, a Tanzanian, stated in his article, "Nyerere vs. Nkrumah: Why Did East African Federation Initiative Collapse in 1963?":

"A treaty establishing the East African Community was finally ratified in 1999 and took effect in 2000. The journey towards East African political Federation reached a milestone in April of 2014 when the heads of state decided to start the process of drafting a constitution for political federation.

This was not the first time that East African leaders came to the table with the goal of establishing a Federation. The heads of state from Kenya, Uganda, and Tanganyika, signed the Declaration of Federation on June 5, 1963. The initiative never came to fruition as both internal and external factors led to the collapse of the negotiations.

While there was a fair share of blame on all the parties involved, there is one particular factor for the collapse of the 1963 East African Federation initiative that deserves closer scrutiny: the role of Ghana in killing the East African Federation.

Two giants emerged on the African political scene of

the early 1960s: Kwame Nkrumah of Ghana and Julius K. Nyerere of Tanzania. The two were staunch proponents of Pan-Africanism, an ideology and a movement that encourages the solidarity of Africans in Africa and around the world.

Nkrumah and Nyerere ultimately wanted to see continental unity and the establishment of a 'United States of Africa.' However, by the end of 1961, the two differed on the approaches to achieving their common goal of unifying Africa.

Nkrumah called for the immediate establishment of the 'United States of Africa.' Nyerere on the other hand, argued that the best approach is a regional approach. Build regional unity first and eventually bring them together to create a 'United States of Africa.' This approach, Nyerere would argue, was more practical.

The quest for African unity remains elusive a little more than 50 years later.

There is a raging debate on whose approach was correct. On one side, there are those who blame the adherents of regional approach for the decision to reject Nkrumah's proposal at the first and second OAU Summits. They argue that the Second OAU conference in Cairo was the last nail in the coffin for any hopes of building continental unity. These pundits point to the failure of the regional attempts to build unity as an example of the futility of such initiatives.

This debate exhumes passion from adherents of both sides. While Nkrumah's call for an immediate establishment of the 'United States of Africa' was never given a chance, it must be pointed out that regional political Federation was never given an opportunity to be tested either.

Nkrumah started as a staunch supporter of building regional unity. He called for regional Federation in 1953. He worked diligently to establish West African Federation in the 1950s after Ghana (then Gold Coast) won self-government. The initiative eventually failed.

Nkrumah was briefly successful with the Ghana-Guinea Union of 1958. The two countries were joined by Mali in 1961 to form the Union of Ghana, Guinea, and Mali.

The Union faced many challenges from the outset. The Union of the three countries failed by the end of 1961.

Nyerere came to view regional unity as the correct path for building African unity in the end of the 1950s. Nyerere and Tom Mboya of Kenya discussed the idea of building regional unity in 1958 after returning from Ghana's first independence anniversary celebrations. The two East African leaders decided to establish a Pan African regional body to bring together independence movements from the region to share ideas, resources, and build unity.

Nyerere was the only one in position to establish such an organization. TANU had just won the first Legislative Council elections and it was clear that self-government was within reach. Thus in September of 1958, Tanganyika leaders called a conference in Mwanza that led to the establishment of Pan African Freedom Movement for East and Central Africa (PAFMECA). Delegates came from Malawi, Zambia, Rwanda and Burundi, Uganda, Kenya, and Zanzibar.

One of the agendas discussed at the conference was the question of Federation. A decision was made to postpone the issue of Federation until a later date. It was decided that the question of Federation should be revisited once the territories had advanced towards independence and won self-government.

The idea of Federation was forefront in Nyerere's plans for east Africa. The victory of 1958 and 1959 elections guaranteed that Tanganyika would win self-government soon. This victory indicated to Nyerere that the time was ripe to start campaigning for East African Federation.

He announced through BBC London on January 1, 1960 his desire to see Tanganyika, Kenya, and Uganda join together in a Federation. Nyerere then took his case to the Conference of Independent African States in Ethiopia in June of 1960. He announced his willingness to delay Tanganyika's independence up to six months to allow for the formation of East African Federation.

Nkrumah and Nyerere, the two African giants, followed a similar path, but at different times.

Nkrumah announced in 1953 after the Gold Coast won self-government that he wanted to see the 'amalgamation of territories on a regional basis and methods of progress towards an ultimate Pan-African Commonwealth of Free, Independent United States of Africa.'

This quest remained unattainable as each territory moved closer to independence in West Africa Nkrumah's failure to build regional unity would eventually convince him to bitterly oppose any such attempts elsewhere.

Nyerere moved full force after 1960 in his quest to establish East African Federation. He took the case to the PAFMECA Conference in Mbale, Uganda in December of 1960. Nyerere tabled a memorandum entitled 'East African Federation (Freedom and Unity)' for discussion and approval. He continued to push for Federation with Kenya, Uganda, and Zanzibar leaders between 1961 and 1962.

Nkrumah changed his mind by late 1961 on the merits of a regional approach to build African unity. He not only came to view regional approach as wrong, he came to see it as a serious threat to the quest for building African unity. He would argue that regional groupings were part of 'Balkanization of Africa,' borrowing from a 19th century saying that described the disintegration into smaller territories of the Balkans in Eastern Europe. According to Nkrumah, regional groups were a major threat to the quest for establishing the 'United States of Africa.'

Efforts to speed up the process towards East African Federation increased in the course of 1962. Nyerere lobbied with his counterparts in Uganda and Kenya. He published an article in March of 1963 entitled 'A United

States of Africa.' The article was the most explicit explanation of his vision for a united Africa.

Nyerere argued eloquently that Africa must unite. He asserted, 'For the sake of all African states, large or small, African unity must come and it must be real unity,' and added, 'Our goal must be a United States of Africa.' As for the approach, Nyerere argued 'This goal must be achieved, and it does not matter whether this is done by one step or by many...' Nyerere was committed to building a 'United States of Africa.'

The situation in African scene was tense in the first half of 1963. To make matters worse, tension between Tanganyika and Ghana increased after the assassination of the President of Togo, Sylvanus Olympio on January 13, 1963.

Nyerere sat with his hands on his head and wept after announcing the assassination of President Olympio. The assassination shocked many African leaders. Tanganyika did not hide its suspicion that Ghana played a role in the assassination. Ghana and Togo were involved in a tug of war over its borders. Nkrumah had laid claims to parts of Togo.

It was partly in reaction to this crisis and the assassination of President Olympio that Tanganyika would take a strong position at the First OAU Summit in Ethiopia in 1963 on the issue of respecting existing borders and not interfering in the internal affairs of other countries. This, some critics have argued, killed any hopes of achieving continental unity. But did it? What of regional approach? What happened to that initiative?

Nyerere and Nkrumah clashes became more pronounced at the First OAU Summit in Ethiopia. Oscar Kambona, Tanganyika Foreign Minister, was selected as the chairman of the powerful Political Committee. The decision by the majority of African leaders to give that important position to a Tanganyikan instead of a Ghanaian, was telling. The decision gave some indication on where the majority of African leaders stood on the Nyerere Vs. Nkrumah dispute.

In the end, Kambona played a major role in shaping the final OAU charter.

This was the first blow to Nkrumah. Another blow to Nkrumah was the decision by the OAU to exclude Ghana from the Committee of Nine (African Liberation Committee). Nkrumah took umbrage at the decisions made by the OAU in May and June of 1963 that excluded his country.

The move towards East African Federation showed most promise in June of 1963 when Jomo Kenyatta, Milton Obote, and Nyerere agreed to work on establishing the East African Federation. It was at this point that the opposition to the Federation initiative by Ghana went from rhetoric into action.

Ghana organized a campaign to sabotage the East African Federation. The efforts concentrated in Uganda. But efforts were also made by Ghana to convince Kenya, Zambia and Malawi leaders to reject Federation. The focal point of the campaign centered on Uganda.

The clash between Nkrumah and Nyerere reached its apex after East African leaders issued the Declaration of Federation. Nkrumah moved with full force to torpedo the initiative. He wrote 'Having accepted a common destiny for Africa at Addis Ababa, we can no longer stand aloof in the fact of any danger that threatens our common cause. It is for this reason that I have been compelled to express my own apprehensions concerning the proposal to unite East African States into a single political entity.'

Nkrumah would claim that the scheme would build regional royalty and frustrate any hopes of a continental unity. He also expressed worries that the East African Federation was an imperialist scheme because it received support of the West. There could only be one solution for him: take action to kill the East African initiative. This Nkrumah did skillfully.

Obote, Nyerere, and Kenyatta issued the Federation Declaration on June 5, 1963. The Declaration stated:

'We, the leaders of the people and governments of East Africa... pledge ourselves to the political federation of East Africa. Our meeting today is motivated by the spirit of Pan-Africanism, and not by mere selfish regional interests. ... We believe that the East African Federation can be a practical step towards the goal of Pan-African unity. We share a common past, and are convinced of our common destinies.'

This Nairobi agreement was the closest East African leaders would come to establishing a Federation.

The position of Uganda would change drastically in the months to come leading to the collapse of the negotiations.

About two months after the Declaration was issued, Nyerere would tell an American diplomat that Uganda was pulling out of the agreement they signed in June of 1963. Nyerere told the diplomat that the problem was not with the concept of Federation itself, but that Uganda leaders were making frivolous demands such as the site of the capital and demands for jobs.

What was the cause of this policy reversal?

Part of the explanation lies with external influences on Uganda stemming from Ghana. Nkrumah told the Ghana National Assembly on June 21, 1963 that the 'idea of a political federation of East Africa' was supported by the British government because they wanted to be 'sure of retaining their rapidly waning influence in Africa.'

Nkrumah dispatched his most skillful lieutenants to East and Central Africa. He concentrated his efforts in Uganda where Milton Obote was one of his greatest admirers. He sent Busumtwi-Sam to Uganda. Nkrumah also dispatched A.K. Barden, the former head of the powerful Africa Bureau, to East Africa. Barden, a former police, had recruited police into the Bureau and ran successful operations.

Ghana High Commission in Tanganyika was reduced to a handful of people after June of 1963 as tension between Tanganyika and Ghana rose. Some of the Ghanaian diplomats were transferred from Tanganyika to Uganda.

The Government of Ghana poured money into Uganda between 1962 and 1963. Paulo Muwanga, Ugandan MP, received $39,000 from Ghana in 1963 to start farmer's council in Uganda.

Ghanaian funds were also funneled to Uganda through trade unions. For example, the Uganda Federation of Labor had cozy relations with Ghana labor and farmer's unions AATUF and AAFU. Ghana gave tens of thousands of dollars to the Uganda labor union UFL. It is not surprising that UFL took the Ghana view of the immediate establishment of 'United States of Africa.'

The *Times of UK* reported in September 1963 that Nkrumah was 'bitterly opposed to an East African Federation and is influential with Mr. Obote..'

One of the most telling examples of Obote's close relations to Nkrumah took place after Obote married Miria Kalule in November of 1963. Ghana Air Force plane was sent to pick up the newly weds to fly to Accra for their honeymoon.

It cannot be denied that the Ugandan position could have come from the conviction that immediate establishment of continental unity was the best approach, yet it would be injudicious to dismiss the possibility that the large sums of money handed to the Ugandan leaders did not influence their views.

Obote and Benedicto Kiwanuka came to oppose the East African Federation initiative.

The reasons given by Uganda leaders for the opposition after signing the Federation Declaration varied from frivolous to serious concerns. For example, Adoko Nekyon, Uganda delegate to the East African Federation negotiations and Obote's brother in-law, demanded that each country should have a separate foreign representation. There were also fears that Uganda's trade surplus and balanced budget would crumble once they united with their neighbors.

The Ugandans claimed to be in support of East African Federation, but raised some of the above issues to say it would not work out for them.

The negotiations for political Federation reached a stalemate. Numerous subsequent attempts were made to revive the talks; such attempts were eventually unsuccessful.

The resistance from Uganda after July of 1963 led Nyerere to conclude that there were external interference that led to the change of heart by Uganda. Nyerere told an American diplomat in August of 1963 that 'various external influences' were at work in Kampala.

Talks continued and eventually an agreement was reached for the establishment of the East African Community that lasted from 1967 to 1977; however, the grand scheme of an East African political Federation was never given an opportunity to be established and tested. Like Nkrumah's continental unity initiative, Nyerere's attempt to build regional unity through Federation was also never given a chance.

In a speech given in January of 1964, Nyerere would pronounce:

'The Challenges of the 20th century is the conversion of nationalism into internationalism.'

This is a challenge that remains elusive in the 21st century.

It remains to be seen if East African leaders will rise to the challenge and make the dream of a united East Africa a reality. This dream must include measures to build continental unity. For it is with the 'United States of Africa'

that the hopes of a vibrant and flourishing Africa lies." –
(Azaria Mbughuni, *Business Times*, Dar es Salaam,
Tanzania, 3 October 2014; Taifaletu: Politics, Society &
Things).

Also, the Marxism Nkrumah advocated, suited to
African conditions, did not last in Ghana; nor did
Nyerere's *ujamaa*, derived from the traditional way of life
and developed into a national ideology.

It is equally true that Nkrumah's political thought can
not be understood without understanding the role
Marxism-Leninism played in the evolution of his thinking;
it played no role in the case of Nyerere.

And like Nyerere, Nkrumah remains one of the most
admired leaders in the history of post-colonial Africa; he is
also one of the most controversial. But both are giants in
African and world history. As Professor Mazrui stated:

"Julius Nyerere is the most enterprising of African
political philosophers. He has philosophized extensively in
both English and Kiswahili.

He has tried to tear down the language barriers
between ancestral cultural philosophy and the new
ideological tendency of the post-colonial era.

Nyerere is superbly eloquent in both English and
Kiswahili. He has allowed the two languages to enrich
each other as their ideas have passed through his intellect.

His concept of *ujamaa* as a basis of African socialism
was itself a brilliant cross-cultural transition. *Ujamaa*
traditionally implied *ethnic* solidarity. But Nyerere
transformed it from a dangerous principle of ethnic
nepotism into more than a mere equivalent of the
European word 'socialism.'

In practice his socialist policies did not work – as much
for global reasons as for domestic. But in intellectual
terms Nyerere is a more original thinker than Kwame
Nkrumah – and linguistically much more innovative.

Nkrumah tried to update Lenin – from Lenin's *Imperialism: The Highest Stage of Capitalism* to Nkrumah's *Neo-Colonialism: The Last Stage of Imperialism.* Nyerere translated Shakespeare into Kiswahili instead – both *Julius Caesar* and *The Merchant of Venice.*

Nkrumah's exercise in Leninism was a less impressive cross-cultural achievement than Nyerere's translation of Shakespeare into an African language.

Yet both these African thinkers will remain among the towering figures of the twentieth century in politics and thought." – (Ali A. Mazrui in Ali. A. Mazrui, ed., *General History of Africa VIII: Africa Since 1935*, Berkeley, California, USA: University of California Press, 1993, p. 674; Ali A. Mazrui, *African Thought in Comparative Perspective*, Newcastle upon Tyne: Cambridge Scholars Publishing, 2014, p. 22).

Union of African States under a Federal Government: A Dream Deferred

NKRUMAH and Nyerere were some of the most prominent leaders who played a major part in forming the Organisation of African Unity in Addis Ababa, Ethiopia, in May 1963.

The Casablanca Group (of radicals), of which Ghana was a member, and the Monrovia Group (of moderates) reached a compromise on what kind of organisation African leaders should form in the quest for continental unity.

The Pan-African Freedom Movement for East and Central Africa (PAFMECA) formed at a conference held from 16 – 18 September 1958 in the port town of Mwanza on the shores of Lake Victoria in northern Tanganyika under the leadership of Nyerere three years before he led his country to independence also played a major role in laying the foundation for the formation of the Organisation of African Unity.

It was also Nyerere who was responsible for one of the resolutions resolution which became one of the cardinal principles of the OAU when the organisation was formed. He presented a resolution which stated that African countries should maintain the boundaries they inherited at independence to avoid chaos and conflict which could result from any attempt to change those borders as Somalia attempted to do by claiming Djibouti, parts of northeastern Kenya and the Ogaden region of Ethiopia which were mostly inhabited by ethnic Somalis in order to create Greater Somalia. As Nyerere himself stated:

"In 1964 we went to Cairo to hold, in a sense, our first summit after the inaugural summit. I was responsible for moving that resolution that Africa must accept the borders which we inherited from colonialism; accept them as they are. The resolution was passed by the organisation (OAU) with two reservations: one from Morocco, another from Somalia." – (Nyerere, "Reflections," in Godfrey Mwakikagile, *Nyerere and Africa: End of an Era*, 2010, p. 556).

Like Somalia, Morocco also had territorial ambitions of annexation. The Moroccan king claimed what was then Spanish Sahara to be an integral part of Morocco.

Despite its good intentions, Nkrumah did not like the resolution that was presented by Nyerere to maintain the territorial integrity of African countries. He saw it as a deliberate attempt to keep Africa balkanised if the countries continued to maintain their sovereignties instead of submerging them in a larger entity under one government - of a United States of Africa - as he strongly urged his colleagues to do.

Nkrumah also had ties with some people in Tanzania who tried to undermine Nyerere. One of the Tanzanian leaders who was close to Nkrumah was foreign affairs minister, Oscar Kambona, who was also close to Nyerere but who also had his own ambitions.

Kambona even attended the All African People's Conference in Accra, Ghana, in 1958, organised by Nkrumah. He later became very close to Nkrumah. He maintained close ties with the Ghanaian leader when he was Tanzania's minister of defence and external affairs at a time when Nkrumah was trying hard to undermine Nyerere. Kambona himself was nurturing his own ambition to replace Nyerere as president of Tanzania. Nkrumah tried to accomplish his mission by cultivating ties with some people in the Tanzanian government who were close to Nyerere and who would be willing to work with him against the Tanzanian leader:

"East Africa was high on Nkrumah's list of subversion priorities. At one point, early in 1965, an attempt was made to recruit two sources close to Tanzania's President Julius Nyerere to 'exploit the political contradictions in the East African area.'" – (*Atlas*, a journal, New York: Worley Publishing Company, 1966, p. 22).

Kambona was probably was one of them, considering the close ties he had with Nkrumah and his own ambition to be the next president of Tanzania. He became a bitter opponent of Nyerere after he left Tanzania in July 1967 and was the mastermind of a plot to overthrow the Tanzanian leader. The coup was to take place in October 1969, when Kambona was living in exile in London, but was discovered by Tanzania's intelligence service before it could be carried out.

Under Nyerere, Tanzania had earned credentials as a radical state in pursuit of Pan-Africanist ideals the same way Ghana was under Nkrumah. After Nkrumah was overthrown, Tanzania was the next choice for a number of people who were supporters of Nkrumah but who had to leave Ghana after the military coup. They included freedom fighters from southern Africa who were being trained in Ghana when Nkrumah was in power. They were flown to Dar es Salaam within days of Nkrumah's ouster; some of their expenses - for plane tickets and so on - paid by a number of Afro-Americans living in Accra.

Dar es Salaam was the obvious destination for the freedom fighters who had been expelled from Ghana by the new military regime - which was subservient to the United States in a disgusting way - because it was the headquarters of the OAU Liberation Committee in a country that had been chosen by other African leaders to provide sanctuary for the freedom fighters; a clear acknowledgement of Nyerere's stature as a highly influential leader and strong supporter of the liberation movements in southern Africa.

Nkrumah was also highly respected as a strong supporter of African liberation and as an ardent Pan-Africanist. But he was surpassed by Nyerere in the context of southern Africa. As Professor Mazrui stated in his lecture at the University of Ghana in 2002:

"The torch of African radicalism, after the coup which overthrew Nkrumah in 1966, was in fact passed to Nyerere. The great voice of African self-reliance, and the most active African head of government in relation to liberation in Southern Africa from 1967 until the 1980s was in fact Julius Nyerere." - (Ali A. Mazrui in his lecture "Nkrumahism and The Triple Heritage: Out of the Shadows" at the University of Ghana-Legon in 2002).

Jaramogi Oginga Odinga who, like Milton Obote, was a close friend of Nkrumah, also acknowledged Nyerere's stature as a leading Pan-Africanist and champion of independence and liberation when, after Nkrumah was overthrown, he said Nyerere "is Nkrumah today."

Although the mantle of leadership in terms of Pan-African militancy may have passed on to Nyerere after Nkrumah was ousted in 1966, there is no question that Nyerere had already won tremendous respect from his fellow heads of state on the continent as a leading champion of African liberation and independence when they chose Dar es Salaam to be the headquarters of the

OAU Liberation Committee. That was in 1963, about three years before Nkrumah was overthrown. Therefore, he acquired the mantle of leadership on a continental scale, on his own merits, even when Nkrumah was still in power.

Ghana under Nkrumah ended up being the headquarters of the OAU Defence Committee based in Accra, but important only for its symbolism since it was largely ineffective, unlike the Liberation Committee based in Dar es Salaam. Nkrumah tried strenuously to have Accra chosen by the OAU to be the headquarters of the Liberation Committee but other African leaders chose Dar es Salaam, instead.

Still, it was in acknowledgement of Nyerere's and Nkrumah's stature as giants in the pantheon of Pan-African leadership that their countries were chosen by their colleagues to be the headquarters of the two OAU committees even though one of those committees was important only for its symbolic value – yet a highly significant gesture to Nkrumah as an embodiment of Pan-Africanism and a trail blazer in the African independence struggle when he led the Gold Coast to become the first black African country to emerge from colonial rule; also befitting a leader who, during the Congo crisis in 1960, was the first to propose formation of an African High Command to defend the continent.

Nkrumah's goal was never realised. An African High Command which could also have helped stop conflicts in different parts of the continent was never formed.

Also, unfortunately for Nkrumah, he failed where his rival, Nyerere, succeeded. He formed the Ghana-Guinea Union which Mali later joined to form the Ghana-Guinea-Mali Union. It collapsed. It was a union only on paper. By remarkable contrast, Nyerere succeeded in uniting Tanganyika with Zanzibar to form Tanzania. Nyerere also was on the way to forming an East African federation which Nkrumah strongly opposed. He played a significant role in blocking formation of an East African federation which Nyerere would probably have presided over in the following years. Nkrumah did his best to make sure Nyerere did not succeed in his venture. But he did not stop there.

He took his crusade against Nyerere to the OAU summit in Cairo in July 1964 where he hoped to mobilise support for his attempt to portray Nyerere as someone who was an obstacle to continental unity under one government because he wanted to form an East African federation which Nkrumah claimed would only be balkanisation of Africa on a grand scale.

He also wanted to portray Nyerere as someone who was not qualified to host and help train freedom fighters from the countries, especially those in southern Africa, which were still under white minority rule.

Tanganyika had been chosen by other African leaders to be the headquarters of the OAU Liberation Committee when they first met in Addis Ababa, Ethiopia, to form the Organisation of African Unity. Nkrumah did not like that.

At the OAU summit in Cairo, Nyerere responded to Nkrumah's criticism and attacks by saying "Some people insist on African unity now, not because they care at all, but because they hope that some stupid historian in the future" will praise them for being the first to seek continental unity when others did not, thus getting satisfaction from being glorified as true Pan-Africanists; it was all for personal glory.

Professor Willard Scott Thompson, a renowned American scholar - John F. Kennedy once said Thompson would be president of the United States someday - provided a different version of what happened at the OAU summit in Cairo. He contended that Nyerere misunderstood Nkrumah. He stated that when Nkrumah said "an imperialist agent," he was not talking about Nyerere; he was talking about Congo-Leopoldville, a country in turmoil during that period because of foreign intervention, where it had once been suggested freedom fighters should be trained. As he stated in his book, *Ghana's Foreign Policy, 1957 – 1966: Diplomacy Ideology, and the new State*:

"In Cairo, when Nkrumah had persisted in raising the issue of union government through back door and side door, despite continual defeat, Senghor had commented: 'I think we have already pronounced ourselves on the fact that we cannot, at present, form a Pan-African government'....

Botsio (Ghana's minister of foreign affairs Kojo Botsio) arrived in Cairo in mid-July for the foreign ministers' meeting, with inflexible instructions (from Nkrumah) to press for union government and a high command....

After Nkrumah's attacks on the proposed East African federation and what Nyerere thought was an accusation that Tanganyika was an imperialist agent, he decided that enough damage had been done. In the sessions remaining before his own speech he was seen writing, obviously recasting his speech.

According to Botsio, Nkrumah's own speech had been reconstructed in part at the last minute; thus several references in it were ambiguous. As one result, Nyerere misread Nkrumah's attack on the (OAU) liberation committee (based in Dar es Salaam). Nyerere was right in saying that the only reason Ghana had criticized the committee was that the Addis Ababa conference 'had committed the unforgivable crime of not including Ghana on the Committee.' Nkrumah – and Nyerere quoted – had said:

'The choice of the Congo as a training base for freedom fighters was a logical one and there was every reason to accept the offer of the Congolese Government to provide offices and accommodation for the representatives of the Liberation *Committee* [i.e. Movements]. Africa's freedom fighters should not, however, have been exposed to the espionage, intrigues, frustrations and disappointments which they have experienced in the last 8 months. What would be the result of entrusting the training of freedom fighters against imperialism into the hands of an imperialist agent?'

Nyerere incorrectly concluded that Nkrumah believed that the headquarters of the liberation *committee* should have been in Léopoldville, and had instead been located in Dar-es-Salaam, a place of 'espionage and intrigue' (with freedom fighters trained, at that, by an 'imperialist agent'). Nkrumah had referred only to the Congo in this section of his speech, and had meant to say 'Liberation *Movements*,' as indicated in the quoted passage.

His mistake made Nyerere's misunderstanding natural, although Nyerere's reading of it is contradicted on internal evidence.

Yet there was enough in Nkrumah's speech that Nyerere did get right to make this confusion almost negligible; certainly most African governments at the time were not interested in the clarification....

The official version of Nkrumah's speech, 'The Quest for a United Africa,' Accra, 1964 (printed after the conference), uses the word 'MOVEMENTS' at the crucial passage. There is no question that Nkrumah meant 'movements,' by all accounts. Nkrumah obviously knew the 'committee' was headquartered in Dar....

According to Botsio, Nyerere later apologized for the misunderstanding, but according to Tanzanian sources, the apology was only directed to the specific point, not to the substance of the speech." – (Willard Scott Thompson, *Ghana's Foreign Policy, 1957 – 1966: Diplomacy Ideology, and the new State,* op. cit., pp. 350, 352, 353. See also Nkrumah's speech in Cairo in July 1964 when he criticised the OAU Liberation Committee and when he talked about "an imperialist agent," quoted in BBC, IV, No. 1611, 22 July 1964, cited by W.S. Thompson, ibid., p. 352).

By that time, when the African leaders met in Cairo in July 1964, Nyerere had already been entrusted with the training of the freedom fighters the previous year when the OAU chose Tanzania to be the headquarters of the OAU Liberation Committee. Therefore, it is easy to understand why Nkrumah seemed to be talking about Nyerere, and not a Congolese leader in Leopoldville, when he said Africa should not trust "an imperialist agent" to be in charge of the training of the freedom fighters.

It seemed he was not talking about President Joseph Kasavubu. May be he was talking about Moise Tshombe who was prime minister of Congo-Leopoldville under Kasavubu during that time when he gave his speech at the OAU summit in Cairo, talking about "an imperialist agent"; which Tshombe was. Nkrumah himself had earlier, on 12 August 1960, written Tshombe about Tshombe's collaboration with the imperialists in destroying Congo. As he stated in the letter:

"You have assembled in your support the foremost advocates of imperialism and colonialism in Africa and the most determined opponents of African freedom. How can you, as an African, do this?" - (Nkrumah, in his letter to Moise Tshombe, 12 August 1960, reproduced in Ghana Government's White Paper, No. 6/60, p. 8, Accra, Ghana, August 1960; and in A. Mazrui, *Towards A Pax Africana*, op. cit., p. 38).

Nyerere also called Tshombe a traitor. As he stated in his address to the National Assembly of the United Arab Republic in Cairo on 9 April 1967:

"It is not possible for African states to compromise on the basic principles of African freedom and African equality. A leader like Tshombe, who was willing to employ South African racialists in order to maintain his own power, and who was willing to dismember an African state if he could not control it – such a man could obviously not bring his nation into a coherent African entity.

But the reason is not that his economic policies involved compromise with the exploiters of Africa. The reason is his deliberate betrayal of the basic principles of African freedom and African equality. To negotiate with such a man would be equivalent to negotiating with the present regime in South Africa." - (Nyerere, "A New Look at Conditions for Unity," *Freedom and Socialism*, op. cit., pp. 295 – 296).

Other observers such as Ali Mazrui, unlike Professor Thompson, reached the same conclusion Nyerere did – that when Nkrumah talked about "an imperialist agent" being entrusted with the training of the freedom fighters, he was talking about Nyerere since the freedom fighters were based in Tanzania, not in Congo.

And the fact that Nkrumah changed parts of his speech at the last minute, resulting in several ambiguous references in the text, seems to suggest that the ambiguity was deliberate, intended to cause some confusion and cast doubt on Nyerere as a true Pan-Africanist and portray him as "an imperialist agent" despite all the evidence to the contrary, especially when Tanzania had already been chosen to be the headquarters of all the African liberation movements.

Also, there was a major difference between the two leaders – Nkrumah and Nyerere – in the way they pursued continental unity, which was partly fuelled by their adversarial relationship although they also worked together on a number of major issues more than they did with other African leaders with the exception of Nasser, Ben Bella, Sekou Toure and Modibo Keita who were also their ideological compatriots and close friends – members of a secret group within the OAU known as "The Group of Six," according to what Ben Bella said in an interview in Geneva, Switzerland, in 1995.

Unlike most African leaders, Nkrumah wanted immediate continental unification; Nyerere preferred the regional approach and said several times - before, during, and after the Cairo summit - that he agreed with Nkrumah on the need for a continental government but it could not be established immediately. In fact, he was one of the very few leaders - together with Nkrumah, Sekou Toure, Modibo Keita and Sourou-Migan Apithy - who strongly believed African countries should unite under one government.

Also, Nkrumah did not want the OAU Liberation Committee to be based in the country of his rival – although his ideological compatriot as well – Nyerere; hence his scathing criticism of both Nyerere and the Committee. As Professor William Burnett Harvey stated in his book, *Law and Social Change in Ghana*:

"The signing of the O.A.U. Charter abated the sharpness of the Casablanca-Monrovia split without removing the underlying causes. The continuing divisions were dramatically illustrated by the acid exchange between Dr. Nkrumah and President Nyerere of Tanganyika and Zanzibar at the Heads of State meeting in Cairo in July, 1964.

The clash was precipitated by an address by Dr. Nkrumah urging immediate establishment of a United Government of Africa; in this speech he attacked the performance of the Liberation Committee established at Addis Ababa to assist the 'Freedom Fighters' in the still-dependent territories.

According to Dr. Nkrumah, the Freedom Fighters had

been exposed to 'espionage, intrigues, frustrations and disappointments,' had been denied food, clothing and medicine and proper facilities for training. He complained that the Congo (Leopoldville) rather than Tanganyika was the 'logical' training base for Freedom Fighters. In a curious rhetorical question he asked, 'What could be the result of entrusting the training of Freedom Fighters against imperialism into the hands of an imperialist agent?' For all these ills, Nkrumah found the cure in the immediate establishment of a United Government of Africa.

Dr. Nyerere responded with understandable heat. He pointed out that Ghana was the only country that had made no financial contribution to the work of the Liberation Committee; he insisted that Ghana's failure to contribute had not resulted from the inadequate performance of the Committee but that the decision had in fact been made at Addis Ababa when Ghana was not given membership on the Committee and Dar es Salaam had been chosen as the Committee's headquarters.

Dr. Nyerere declared that he was becoming increasingly convinced that the African states were divided 'between those who genuinely want a Continental Government and will work patiently for its realization; and those who simply use a phrase 'Union Government,' for the purposes of propaganda.' Clearly in his judgment, Ghana fell into the latter category.

Dr. Nyerere did 'not believe that there is a choice between achieving African unity step by step and achieving it in one act. The one-act choice is not available to us except in some curious imagination.'" - (William Burnett Harvey, *Law and Social Change in Ghana*, Princeton, New Jersey, USA: Princeton University Press, 1966, p. 169).

Also, Nkrumah's determination to block formation of an East African federation not only tarnished his image; it enhanced Nyerere's credentials as a realist in the quest for continental unity. As Nyerere put it: "When you set out to build a house, you don't begin by putting on the roof; first you start by laying the foundations." And according to Professor Mazrui:

"Nyerere...denounced Nkrumah's attempt to deflate the East African federation movement as petty mischief-making arising from Nkrumah's own sense of frustration in his own Pan-African ventures....

He went public with his attack on Nkrumah. He referred to people who pretended that they were in favour of African continental union when all they cared about was to ensure that 'some stupid historian in the future' praised them for being in favour of the big continental ambition before anyone else was willing to undertake it....

On balance, history has proved Nkrumah wrong on the question of Nyerere's commitment to liberation. Nyerere was second to none in that commitment.

At that Cairo conference of 1964 Nkrumah had asked 'What could be the result of entrusting the training of Freedom Fighters against imperialism into the hands of an imperialist agent?'

In the debates between incremental Pan-Africanism and rapid unification Nkrumah found a rival in Julius K. Nyerere of Tanzania....Nkrumah and Nyerere had already begun to be rivals as symbols of African radicalism before the coup which overthrew Nkrumah. Nkrumah was beginning to be suspicious of Nyerere in this regard....

The two most important issues over which Nyerere and Nkrumah before 1966 might have been regarded as rivals for continental pre-eminence were the issues of African liberation and African unity." - (Ali A. Mazrui in his lecture "Nkrumahism and The Triple Heritage: Out of the Shadows" at the University of Ghana-Legon in 2002. See also Nyerere, "When you set out to build a house,..." at the OAU summit, Cairo, Egypt, July 1964, quoted by Colin

Legum, "The Goal of an Egalitarian Society," in Colin Legum and Geoffrey Mmari, eds., *Mwalimu: The Influence of Nyerere*, op. cit., p. 191).

Professor Mazrui's version that Nkrumah did, indeed, call Nyerere "an imperialist agent" (out of frustration with Nyerere's rise and influence as a continental leader, threatening to eclipse Nkrumah in some respects, after Tanzania was chosen by other African leaders to be the headquarters of the OAU Liberation Committee) also seems to be consistent with the sequence of events before and after the Cairo summit in July 1964 when the two African leaders clashed.

It is also possible Nyerere misunderstood Nkrumah, and that Nkrumah was referring to somebody else in Congo-Leopoldville – probably Prime Minister Moise Tshombe – when he said "an imperialist agent."

But whatever Nkrumah said and meant in the larger context of his speech in Cairo was still consistent with his own image as Africa's leader.

He saw himself as Africa's pre-eminent leader who did not want to be challenged or surpassed by anybody, demonstrated by his determination to undermine Nyerere's attempt to form an East African federation whose success would have earned Nyerere the distinction of being the first champion of regional integration to achieve his goal of helping unite countries under one government. Nkrumah did not want Nyerere to succeed and be surpassed by him in the quest for unity even on a regional scale, while Nkrumah himself had failed to achieve the same goal in West Africa.

A highly influential Nigerian newspaper, the *West African Pilot* founded by Dr. Nnamdi Azikiwe in 1937 and edited by him from 1937 to 1947, even challenged Nkrumah and Nasser for considering themselves to be *the* continental leaders; a point underscored in the paper's editorial in May 1961:

"Until recently it was a tournament between Nasser and Nkrumah but Africa today contains many stars and meteorites, all of them seeking positions of eminence." - (*West African Pilot*, 18 May 1961; see also *West Africa*, London, 6 May 1961, quoted by A. Mazrui, *Towards A Pax Africana*, op. cit., p. 66).

Nkrumah was virtually isolated at the OAU summit in Cairo besides the support he got from Sekou Toure, Modibo Keita, and Sourou-Migan Apithy of Dahomey in his quest for immediate continental unification. But even they, may be with the exception of President Apithy, did not go far enough to satisfy him. The collapse of the Ghana-Guinea-Mali Union, a pet creature of Nkrumah, demonstrated that even the three ideological compatriots – Nkrumah, Toure and Keita – could not work together to transform their union into a functional entity; it was virtually stillborn.

The adversarial relationship between Nkrumah and Nyerere, with regard to liberation and continental unity, was further addressed by Professor Thompson, as was Nkrumah's failure to convince his colleagues to agree to form one continental government:

"What Nyerere stopped by his speech was the politeness about union government. Tanganyika had, as he pointed out, practiced unity by uniting with Zanzibar; less 'preaching' about unity was needed.

He mocked union government as the panacea for every difficulty that Africa encountered, and also added his own invective: 'to cap this whole series of absurdities, after all the wonderful arguments against unity in East Africa, we are now told again, at this very rostrum, that those who are ready should go ahead and unite (as Nkrumah said in his speech). Those who are ready should now go ahead and unite. Now we have the permission to go ahead....If I were a cynic, I would say we of the United Republic of Tanganyika and Zanzibar are ready. I would ask Ghana to join our United Republic. But I am not a cynic.'

Nyerere's suggestion was no less logically compelling than any of the long line of Nkrumah's proposals, and now they were publicly declared to be nonsense. Nyerere had merely said the Emperor wore no clothes....

The speech was also significant as an opening of the sluice-gate for anti-Ghana feelings on many issues throughout Africa, and it signaled the beginning of the last stage of an 'anti-Nkrumah offensive' that was gaining support across the continent.

Nkrumah had been severely humiliated among his peers. Nonetheless,...the (OAU) decided to hold its second conference of heads of state in Accra, as the Ghanaians had suggested....Nkrumah insisted on bringing up union government.

Sékou Touré, the chairman, noted that the committee named at the foreign ministers' session had only asked the heads of state 'to declare itself on principle.' But Nkrumah insisted on pleading his case, and it is interesting to see what he said amidst his peers:

'What I am suggesting...I didn't say we should set out on this table and within five minutes establish a Union Government....My point was this, that it is a central factor in the political life of the African continent, since it is going to be a vital issue let us at least accept in principle the possibility of the establishment of a Union Government of Africa....

But I say let's say that we should start here and then, and get all the functions and I put forward the suggestion also that we have been able to agree in principle to the possibility of the establishment of Union Government in Africa.

I say let's submit it to the...Jurist's Committee...so...what I am saying is...if it is a good idea then what I put forward is this: Let us give a chance to our Jurist's Committee....But I want to make it clear. I didn't come here to say---I know Rome wasn't built in a day but Rome started somewhere before it became Rome.'

Touré, as chairman – and Nkrumah's ally – tried to summarize the argument as logically as possible and Keita even added that the gap that 'had separated our friend...from the majority...was narrowing.' Apithy of Dahomey evoked memories of Nkrumah's 1947 London pan-African gathering which he had attended, and supported Nkrumah, by this time a picture of pathos.

Sir Abubakar (Tafawa Balewa) let them go no further. An African government was a dream, he said, 'Or a nightmare.' Nigeria, for its part, would never surrender its sovereignty. 'This request, Mr. Chairman, is indirectly a vote of no confidence in the Organisation of African Unity. When we started this Organisation only a year ago we were working, progressing and now we are trying to impose something.' Union government might come, so might world government, he said.

The Emperor of Ethiopia, who knew that at this point it was conceding nothing to grant Nkrumah some concession, and who possessed a sense of dignity, sought to blur the distinctions Sir Abubakar and others were making. 'The proposal of His Majesty [said the interpreter] is to examine the draft, not to reject it.' But Cameroun did not want to examine something that could not be implemented 'before five, ten, fifteen, or even twenty years,' and Bourguiba suggested that the appointment of such a committee would reduce the credibility of the OAU." – (Ibid., pp. 353, and 355).

Nkrumah somewhat saw the absurdity of his quest for immediate continental unification and the impractical nature of his proposal, as was clearly demonstrated by the overwhelming opposition he faced at the OAU summits in Cairo in July 1964 and even in his own capital Accra in

October 1965. But he never gave up in spite of the fact that he was virtually isolated at both conferences:

"With almost any issue of concern to the radical African nationalists, Nkrumah might have taken the lead and increased his influence; he did do this with the Rhodesian question. The question of continental union government, however, interested no one.

His urgent messages to his peers asking for coordination and cooperation on such questions as the 1964 Congolese rebellion lost their force, because he insisted on placing his proposals in the framework of the need for union government.

Since its inception Nkrumah had treated the OAU with contempt, partly because of Nkrumah's policy of union government, more importantly because Ghana could not dominate the OAU. At Cairo, Ghana offered Accra as a sight for the 1965 OAU meeting, for understandable reasons of prestige: this would be its first chance to be a part of the organization's 'in-group.'

Yet the choice of Accra posed a dilemma: Could Ghana sponsor a conference of an organization the objectives of which it rejected? This was resolved with the demand, posed almost daily in the Ghanaian press from September 1964 onwards, that the OAU effect a union government in Accra.

Hardly had Accra been selected than Nkrumah began sketching elaborate plans for a conference headquarters, the scope of which led many to conclude that Nkrumah envisaged the new buildings as an African capital. 'Jobs 600,' the remarkable £10,000,000 complex which was to be used for two weeks at the most, made Nkrumah the subject of jokes throughout the world.

But these missed the point. Obviously Ghana could ill-afford the project with the economy in such disrepair although Nkrumah did assume that the project and the conference would be a useful public diversion at a time of stress; the complex more significantly underlined the extent to which Nkrumah counted on the emergence of union government at the conference. Important objectives in the domestic sector were pushed aside, and Nkrumah told one visitor that this was done because they would be irrelevant or redundant when union government was achieved.

According to Botsio, in (an) interview, Nkrumah began at the Cairo conference itself sketching plans for the complex. Botsio himself favored the building of badly needed estate houses to house the delegates, the cost of which would have been one-tenth that of Job 600." – (Ibid., pp. 355, 357 – 358).

Nkrumah's passion for immediate continental unification will always be remembered. It was first demonstrated in a significant way when he wrote a book, *Africa Must Unite*, whose publication coincided with the first meeting of the 32 African heads of state and government who met in Addis Ababa, Ethiopia, in May 1963 and formed the Organisation of African Unity (OAU). He hoped that once they read the book, they would agree with him to unite their countries under one government – right away at that meeting or soon thereafter. They did not.

It was a severe blow to a leader who was a relentless champion of immediate continental unification and who saw himself as the embodiment of Pan-Africanism more than anybody else. As Nyerere said, Nkrumah "had tremendous contempt" for a large number of African leaders. He stated in an interview with Bill Sutherland:

"My differences with Kwame were that Kwame thought there was somehow a shortcut, and I was saying that there was no shortcut. This is what we have inherited, and we'll have to proceed within the limitations that that inheritance has imposed on us.

Kwame thought that somehow you could say, 'Let there be a United States of Africa' and it would happen. I kept saying, 'Kwame, it's a slow process.'

He had tremendous contempt for a large number of leaders of Africa and I said, 'Fine, but they are there. What are you going to do with them? They don't believe as you do – as you and I do – in the need for the unity of Africa. BUT WHAT DO YOU DO? THEY ARE THERE, AND WE HAVE TO PROCEED ALONG WITH EVERYBODY!'

And I said to him in so many words that we're not going to have an African Napoleon, who is going to conquer the continent and put it under one flag. It is not possible.

At the OAU conference in 1963, I was actually trying to defend Kwame. I was the last to speak and Kwame had said this charter has not gone far enough because he thought he would leave Addis with a United States of Africa.

I told him that this was absurd; that it can't happen. This is what we have been able to achieve. No builder, after putting the foundation down, complains that the building is not yet finished. You have to go on building and building until you finish; but he was impatient because he saw the stupidity of the others." - (Julius Nyerere, in Bill Sutherland and Matt Mayer, eds., *Guns and Gandhi in Africa: Pan African Insight on Nonviolence, Armed Struggle, and Liberation*, Africa World Press, 2000. The interview was also reproduced, from the book, by Chambi Chachage, "Excerpt from Interview with Bill Sutherland," Centre for Consciencist Studies and Analyses (CENSCA), 5 September 2008. See also Bill Sutherland in William Minter, Gaily Hovey, and Charles Cobb Jr., eds., *No Easy Victories: African Liberation and American Activists over a Half Century, 1950 – 2000*, New Africa Press, Trenton, New Jersey, USA, 2007).

Even Milton Obote, who was a close friend of Nkrumah, told the Ghanaian leader at the first OAU summit in Addis Ababa in May 1963 – "unity now" under one continental government could not be achieved. As he stated in an interview years later:

"I took a strong Pan African position in favour of a continental union. In May 1963, I arrived in Addis Ababa where the first conference of leaders of newly independent states was going to take place. Africa had been divided between two groups: the Monrovia group composed of conservatives, and the Casablanca group composed of the progressive radicals.

The Monrovia group was opposed to Nkrumah's proposal for an immediate creation of a union government for the whole of Africa. On the first day I arrived, my friend Kwesi Ama, a Ghanaian, came to me and said Kwame Nkrumah, the president of Ghana, wanted to have lunch with me and that I should 'expect a bomb shell.' I had met Kwesi Ama in London. He was my friend and was Nkrumah's ambassador to London.

Nkrumah was the leader of African progressive opinion. We all admired him immensely. I personally admired Nkrumah immensely. He was an illustrious leader. He shaped African liberation and gave Africa a voice in world affairs. He supported liberation struggles all over Africa. So meeting him was a great honour and opportunity. People like Patrice Lumumba, Julius Nyerere, Kenneth Kaunda, all progressive African leaders looked to Nkrumah.

When we sat down to lunch, Nkrumah told me there was no conference. 'You should go back home.' He said the Monrovia group had already sabotaged the conference. I told him that we should not go back home. We should put our case to the conference on the need for African unity. And I told him that as far as I could see, there was possible success if only we could reorganise what we wanted the conference to do. Nkrumah said we wanted All-African Union Government. I told him that given the polarisation, we could not achieve that. Although we could present our case for immediate African political union, we had to be careful because we could not get the majority needed to see it through.

So we had to argue our case as a bargaining tool to get the conference to form an organisation that would work towards the creation of a continental government.

I also told Nkrumah that while a continental union was a great idea, we could not wish it. We had to put in place an organisation to work towards it.

During the conference, Nkrumah made a great speech on the need for a union government for Africa. He called for a constitution for an African continental government, a common market, an African currency, an African monetary zone, an African central bank and an inter-continental communication system.

I stood up in the conference, called for the creation of a strong Pan African executive and an African parliament to which all African governments must be prepared to surrender their sovereignty. This position was supported by Modibo Keita, president of Mali; Sekou Toure, president of Guinea; and the president of Egypt, Gamal Abdel Nasser. All these were my friends.

My call for immediate unity was tactics. We used the Nkrumah stand to bring others opposed to African co-operation to agree that a compromise meant building an organisation to promote the ideals of unity.

Later in the conference, I suggested that since African unity cannot be achieved overnight, let us put in place an organisation to work towards the realisation of that goal. This was a compromise position between 'unity now' and the extreme position by people like President Tsiranana of Malagasy Republic (now Madagascar), Balewa and others against African co-operation.

Then Ahmed Ben Bella of Algeria took to the floor

with a moving call for African liberation. He pledged 10,000 Algerian volunteers to free African nations still under colonial oppression and white minority rule. 'A Charter will be of no value to us,' he said, 'and speeches will be used against us if there is not first created a blood bank for those fighting for independence.'

I stood up and offered Uganda as a training ground for African troops to be used to liberate African countries from colonial rule and white minority rule.

Then Sekou Toure suggested that we fix a date after which 'if colonialism were not ended, African states would expel the colonial powers.'

Leopold Sedar Senghor of Senegal and Nyerere stood up and made strong recommendations on building capacity to liberate the whole of Africa.

Finally we agreed to the formation of the Organisation of African Unity (OAU) whose mandate it was to end colonial rule and work towards unity." - (Milton Obote, an excerpt from "Milton Obote: My Story," a series of interviews in which Obote was interviewed by Ugandan journalist Andrew Mwenda in Lusaka, Zambia, September – October 2004, published in *The Monitor*, Kampala, Uganda, April 2005).

Nkrumah was very impatient, and highly ambitious, in his pursuit of continental unity. And that was one of his biggest mistakes. Even if he did so with good intentions in order to see Africa united, a continent which would be powerful and prosperous as a single political entity, most of his colleagues saw him as someone who was vainglorious and power-hungry, expecting to rule Africa one day. They were not going to help him achieve his goal. They were power-hungry themselves and wanted to remain presidents of their own countries without losing power or being under somebody else even if they remained leaders in a united Africa.

More than 50 years after Nkrumah exhorted his

colleagues to unite their countries under one government, which he hoped he would lead as United Africa's first president, continental unity remains elusive. Even economic integration on a continental scale remains a distant goal. He had an inordinate ambition to be Africa's "saviour" or "messiah"; hence his title, The Osagyefo, The Redeemer, leading Africa in her quest for redemption.

Also, unfortunately for Nkrumah, the books which he *did not* write – but which he claimed he wrote – are the ones which earned him a reputation as a philosopher and an anti-imperialist icon of global stature; a reputation that persists especially in the Pan-African world.

The books which were written by other people for him and which earned him that reputation were *Consciencism: Philosophy and ideology for decolonization and development with particular reference to the African Revolution*, a highly philosophical work written by Dr. Willie Abraham, and *Neo-Colonialism: The Last Stage of Imperialism* written by American and British Marxists as well as other people close to Nkrumah and living in Accra, Ghana, during that period.

Dr. Willie Abraham also inspired one of the most renowned scholars Africa has ever produced, Ali Mazrui, who partly attributed his work, *The Africans: A Triple Heritage*, to the inspiration he drew from Nkrumah's "book,"*Consciencism*. As Mazrui himself stated:

"Kwame Nkrumah also stimulated my vision of Africa as a convergence of three civilizations – Africanity, Islam and Western culture. Nkrumah called that convergence 'Consciencism.' I later called it 'Africa's Triple Heritage.' I was able to elaborate on my own concept in a BBC/PBS television series titled *The Africans: A Triple Heritage* (1986)." – (Ali A. Mazrui in IGCS Reporters, "Ali A. Mazrui, Witness to History?," op. cit.)

Since the book was not written by Nkrumah but by

Willie Abraham, it is appropriate to give Dr. Abraham credit for providing inspiration to one of the most successful documentaries about Africa by another distinguished African, Dr. Mazrui, who gave Nkrumah credit for inspiring him in other areas as well.

Nkrumah himself had been preceded by the Liberian scholar, Dr. Edward Wilmot Blyden, in expounding the concept of Africa's triple heritage – Africanity, Islam and Western civilisation – and may actually have been inspired by him to elaborate on the convergence of these three civilisations as Blyden did in his acclaimed yet controversial book, *Christianity, Islam and The Negro Race*.

In fact, a number of leading Pan-Africanists, including Nkrumah and Padmore, were greatly inspired by Blyden's ideas on unity, emancipation, African identity and heritage, just as Dr. Willie Abraham's works have provided intellectual stimulus for generation of ideas by some of Africa's prominent thinkers such as Nkrumah.

There are questions about the authorship of some of Nkrumah's other works as well, except his first book,*Towards Colonial Freedom: Africa in the Struggle Against World Imperialism* (actually a pamphlet of about 35 pages); his second book, *Ghana: The Autobiography of Kwame Nkrumah* (encouraged by George Padmore and Padmore's partner Dorothy Pizer to write it), *I Speak of Freedom: A Statement of African Ideology, Africa Must Unite, Class Struggle in Africa, Dark Days in Ghana, Voice from Conakry, The Struggle Continues,* and may be others.

All that may have tarnished his reputation as a thinker. But it did not diminish his stature as a continental leader who was respected and admired across Africa because of the kind of leadership he provided as a staunch Pan-Africanist.

Few can match his record as an ardent advocate of continental unity under one government. Not only was he in a class by himself in that respect; no other leader pursued the same goal with the same passion and intensity as he did when he was in power. He was the first and the last. As Nyerere stated in his speech in Accra on Ghana's 40th independence anniversary:

"After Kwame Nkrumah was removed from the African political scene nobody took up the challenge again."

When Nkrumah was overthrown, Nyerere paid tribute to the Ghanaian leader and even offered him asylum in spite of the differences they had on some issues vital to the wellbeing of Africa. Sekou Toure, Modibo Keita and Nasser also offered Nkrumah asylum.

Nyerere refused to recognise the new military rulers who overthrew Nkrumah and even the civilian government of Dr. Kofi Busia, Nkrumah's arch-rival, who served as prime minister from 1969 to 1972.

When his foreign affairs minister, Victor Owusu, came to Dar es Salaam in 1969 in an attempt to win recognition for the new civilian government, he was received at the airport by a low-ranking official from the ministry of foreign affairs; a deliberate snub to the leaders who had replaced Nkrumah.

Owusu, together with Dr. Busia and other opposition leaders mostly from the Ashanti region, was also involved in a plot to assassinate Nkrumah in 1958, just one year after Nkrumah led the Gold Coast to independence and became the country's first prime minister. He was going to be shot at the airport as he was getting ready to leave for a state visit to India.

The plots to assassinate Nkrumah were attributed to his despotic tendencies, ethno-regional rivalries, foreign intrigues by Western governments and intelligence agencies especially of the United States and Britain; and his determination to establish a highly centralised state that was resolutely opposed by the Ashanti who wanted a federal system under which their kingdom would retain its status as a political entity and be recognised as an autonomous unit – Obote faced the same problem from traditional centres of power, especially from the Buganda kingdom, when he decided to establish a unitary state.

Like Nyerere in Tanzania and Obote in Uganda, Nkrumah knew Ghana would be fractured along ethno-regional lines if he did not centralise power under a strong unitary state.

The country had well-established traditional institutions of authority which were regionally entrenched and needed a political party whose nationalist agenda transcended ethno-regional interests and loyalties. Nkrumah was able to provide that kind of leadership when he formed the Convention People's Party (CPP) which mobilised the masses during the struggle for independence and became the ruling party after the country emerged from colonial rule. But it also galvanised its opponents – mostly regionalists – into action, determined to undermine Nkrumah in his effort to consolidate power at the centre. As Professor Kwame Botwe-Asamoah states in his book, *Kwame Nkrumah's Politico-Cultural Thought and Policies*: *An African-Centered Paradigm for the Second Phase of the African Revolution*:

"In Asante, the Asantehene...and the Ashanti Confederacy Council were to form an ethno-regional political party against Nkrumah's unitary form of government in the 1956 general election (just before independence in March 1957). While Nkrumah's CPP was to enjoy strong support among the Ga-Adangbe groups, the Ewes in the Trust territory were also to form an ethnic-based political party in opposition to Nkrumah's CPP. Similarly, a parochial political party was to be built and based among the northern ethnic groups in opposition to Nkrumah's CPP." – (Kwame Botwe-Asamoah, *Kwame*

Nkrumah's Politico-Cultural Thought and Policies: An African Centered Paradigm for the Second Phase of the African Revolution, New York & London: Routledge, 2005, p. 93).

As a nationalist, Nkrumah had many enemies to contend with. As Professor Harcourt Fuller states in his book, *Building the Ghanaian-State: Kwame Nkrumah's Symbolic Nationalism*:

"Nkrumah's stronghold on power, his bitter rivalry with the Asantes and other groups, and the controversial laws that he had passed jailing some of his political rivals made him a target for violence, symbolically and physically.

During his presidency, an Asante man had threatened violence against the construction of a new statue on Nkrumah in Kumasi in 1957, while his Accra statue was actually bombed in 1961. There were also several unsuccessful assassination attempts against Nkrumah himself.

In Dark Days in Ghana, Nkrumah recalled that 'members of the police and Special Branch have been involved in each of the six attacks made on my life, and have frequently ignored, and sometimes aided, the activities of people they knew were plotting to overthrow the government.'

One such assassination attempt occurred nine months after the bombing of his statue in Accra. On August 1, 1962, according to Nkrumah and Milne, a grenade attack orchstrated by 'leading police officers' in collusion with Emmanuel Obetsebi-Lamptey, 'one of the ringleaders in the plot to kill me,' was made on Nkrumah's life in Kulungugu in northern Ghana. During this unsuccessful attack, several people lost their lives, including a child, and 55 people were injured.

Other attempts on and conspiratorial plots against Nkrumah's life and coup schemes were carried out beginning with the bombing of his residence on November 10, 1955, attributed to NLM supporters; in 1958, pinned to various Opposition party officials, including J.B. Danquah, Reginald Reynolds Amponsah, Modesto Apaloo, Joe Appiah, Kofi Busia, and Victor Owusu; and on January 1, 1964, when a policeman stationed at Flagstaff House fired four shots at the president, but missed.

The various assassination attempts gave Nkrumah the motive to arrest his political opponents, as well as those in his own party whom he wanted to purge. Among those arrested were Minister of Presidential Affairs Tawia Adamafio; Foreign Minister Ako Adjei (a member of The Big Six); and Executive Secretary of the CPP Cofie Crabbe." – (Harcourt Fuller, *Building the Ghanaian-State: Kwame Nkrumah's Symbolic Nationalism*, New York: Palgrave Macmillan, 2014. See also Ahmad A. Rahman, *The Regime Change of Kwame Nkrumah: Epic Heroism in Africa and the Diaspora*, New York: Palgrave Macmillan, 2007, p. 171:

"After the fifth attempt to assassinate Nkrumah with bullets or bombs – and the deaths of 30 innocent bystanders and the wounding of over 300 – he signed the Preventive Detention Act on July 18, 1958. Nkrumah stated that the law should not alarm anybody who was not 'attempting to organise violence, terror, or civil war, or who was not acting as a fifth columnist for some foreign power.'

In addition to the dead bodies, Nkrumah's intelligence agents had given him reason to suspect that certain men in the Opposition were engaging in each of these behaviors. Evidence available now proves that this was a correct assessment.

Reginald Reynolds Amponsah and Modesto Apaloo were members of Parliament and leading members of the Opposition who tried to organize an anti-Nkrumah coup in November 1958. A co-conspirator revealed their plot to a

Nkrumah loyalist.

When the police went to Amponsah's house to arrest him, at 1:00 a.m., they found him in the company of Kofi Busia, Joseph Danquah, Joe Appiah, and Victor Owusu. They were the foremost opposition figures in the country....As a unit, these men – without Danquah who died in 1965 – immediately identified with the new neo-colonial military regime soon after Nkrumah's overthrow").

The military coup against Nkrumah was preceded by a series of assassination attempts on the Ghanaian leader which began as far back as 1955; threats which may explain why he took draconian measures – non-violent – to curb the opposition and protect himself. No leader takes such threats lightly.

The opposition comprised the National Liberation Movement (NLM), the Northern People's Party (NPP) and the United Party (UP).

Nkrumah became Leader of Government Business in 1951 in preparation for independence a few years later.

Most of the attempts to assassinate Nkrumah involved bombings which claimed many innocent lives. The people who wanted to eliminate the Ghanaian leader did not target him alone.

They knew the bombs and grenades they used in public places in an attempt to kill him would claim other lives, collateral damage his political enemies felt was justified even if they did not get their intended target, as long as there was a chance for him to get killed as well. Sometimes the bombings were as indiscriminate as they were bloody. No other Ghanaian leader has been the target of so much violence:

"Systematic assassination attempts on his life as well as terrorism became the language of his political opponents....(He became the target of) the most violent attacks on any president and members of his youth movement in the annals of Ghana.

While Nkrumah was resting and working from his house with his secretary and others because of a terrible cold on the evening of November 10, 1955, the house was bombed.

Between 1955 and 1958 there were several more assassination attempts on his life. Also, there was another plan to shoot him at the airport, as he was about to depart for a state visit to India.

On July 7, 1961, two bombs exploded in Accra, one wrecking Nkrumah's statue in front of the Parliament House.

The most dreadful of all the attempts on Nkrumah's life was the one that occurred at Kulungugu on August 1, 1962. Nkrumah was returning from a state visit to Upper Volta, now Burkina Faso, and had got out from his car to speak to the school children among the crowd who had gathered to greet him, when a bomb contained in a bouquet carried to him by a schoolgirl exploded. 'It killed several and injured many others. Nkrumah sustained serious injury.'

The victims' bodies bled from cuts caused by the splinters from the bomb. Nkrumah was rushed to the nearest hospital for surgery. In the process, Nkrumah refused to have any device to deaden his pain while the operation went on (*Forward Ever*: 47).

In August and September 1961, there were two separate bomb explosions on Nkrumah's life. On September 9, 1962, another bomb exploded near the 'Flagstaff House, the official residence of the President, when the Ghana Young Pioneers Orchestra Band was entertaining the audience to modern Ghanaian Music' (Tetteh, 1999: 104). This explosion killed one person and injured others.

On September 18, 1962, two bombs again went off in Accra killing and injuring several people. One of these bomb blasts occurred in Lucas House in Accra, where nine children fell dead on the spot as their intestines gushed out of their bodies (Ibid: 104). This was followed by another bomb explosion on September 22, 1962. Consequently, a state of emergency on Accra and Tema with dusk to dawn curfew was declared.

Again, another bomb exploded on January 23, 1963, at a CPP rally in Accra Sports Stadium shortly after President Nkrumah had left the scene. This explosion killed over 20 people and more than four hundred people were injured; among the victims were children of the Young Pioneers movement (McFarland & Owusu-Ansah: ixi).

The question is, why the repeated bomb throwing at the Ghana Young Pioneers? In the words of Tetteh, the anti-Nkrumah forces saw in the Young Pioneers movement 'the source of permanent power if allowed to last for at least one generation or 35 years' (Tetteh: 93).

Having failed in their attempts to assassinate Nkrumah through the bomb blasts, the Opposition, including senior police officers, posted a police officer, Seth Ametewe, on guard duty at the Flagstaff House on January 1, 1964, to shoot him. Nkrumah recounts the incident as follows:

'It was at 1 P.M. in the garden of the Flagstaff House. I was leaving the office to go for lunch when four shots were fired at me by one of the policemen on guard duty. He was not a marksman, though his fifth shot succeeded in killing Salifu Dagarti, a loyal security officer who had run towards the would-be assassin as soon as he spotted him among the trees. The policeman then rushed at me, trying to hit me with his rifle butt. I wrestled with him and managed to throw him to the ground and to hold him there on his back until help came, but not before he had bitten me on the neck (Nkrumah, 1968: 41).'

Eventually, the repeated assassination attempts on his life caused Nkrumah to remain 'alone within himself' (Kanu: 40)." – (K. Botwe-Asamoah, *Kwame*

Nkrumah's Politico-Cultural Thought and Policies:, op. cit., pp. 14 – 15).

Nkrumah also said he was able to subdue the policeman (a constable) who tried to kill him at Flagstaff House because he knew some judo techniques.

Nkrumah's opponents who tried to kill him not only supported the new military rulers; they admitted their involvement in various assassination plots to eliminate the Ghanaian leader. As Kwame Botwe-Asamoah states:

"After Nkrumah's overthrow, many in the opposition party admitted having been involved in the assassination attempts on his life.

During the Exemption Committee's hearings, Obetsebi Lamptey's name came out as having been involved in organizing several bomb explosions which caused 'the death of thirty innocent people and seriously injured many others'.

Prior to these acts of terrorism, there had been an abortive coup on November 28, 1958, carried out by Major Awhaitey; the coup was planned by R.R. Amponsah, who later became Minister of Trade in Busia's government, and others in the opposition party, to seize Nkrumah and certain members of his cabinet." – (Ibid., p. 15).

Nkrumah was overthrown nine years after he led the Gold Coast to become the first black African country to win independence. The CIA skillfully used his opponents to facilitate the coup which was masterminded by Howard T. Bane, the CIA station chief in Accra.

Nkrumah was the second member of The Group of Six to be overthrown, preceded by Ben Bella. Modibo Keita was next. He was overthrown in 1968. Nasser died in 1970.

Only two members of the group, Nyerere and Sékou

Touré who were also close friends, remained in power. After Sékou Touré died in 1984, Nyerere was the only member of The Group of Six who remained in power. He lived long enough to witness the end of white minority rule in South Africa in 1994 in a country where Nkrumah, like Nyerere, was also highly regarded as a major inspiration to the freedom fighters and other victims of the abominable institution of apartheid.

Like Nyerere and their colleagues in The Group of Six, Nkrumah would have been thrilled to witness the end of the last white minority government on the continent when the apartheid rulers relinquished power to the black majority after the first democratic elections in the history of South Africa.

Like Nyerere, Nasser, Sékou Touré and Modibo Keita, Ben Bella also would probably have offered Nkrumah asylum but was himself overthrown eight months earlier, in June 1965, before Nkrumah was. Fidel Castro blamed Algeria's minister of foreign affairs, Abdelaziz Bouteflika, for Ben Bella's downfall. Relations between Cuba and Algeria soured as a result of the coup and remained so for several years until Castro softened his attitude towards the new military rulers in Algiers. And as Nyerere stated at a press conference in Dar es Salaam in February 1966 soon after Nkrumah was overthrown:

"What is happening in Africa? What are the coups about? The last few months have seen changes of governments in many African countries. The latest has been in Ghana. What is behind all this? Are these 'revolutions' intended to remove humiliation and oppression from Africa?

Let us take the latest in Ghana. The enemies of Africa are now jubilant. There is jubilation in Salisbury and Johannesburg. Even a fool could begin to wonder whether these 'revolutions' would help Africa.

What was Kwame trying to do? He stood for the

liberation of Africa. There is not a single leader in Africa more committed to this than Kwame. Whom did he anger with his commitment to freedom? Certainly not Africa. He was committed to true independence. He was not merely against ordinary colonialism; he was against neocolonialism – against a colonial power going out through the political door and controlling the country through the economic door." – (Nyerere, quoted by Kwame Nkrumah, *Dark Days in Ghana*, New York: Monthly Review Press, 1968, p. 137; also in *African Quarterly*, Vol. 6, 1967, p. 279; *Pan African Journal*, Vols. 6 – 7, 1973, p. 190; Opoku Agyeman, *Nkrumah's Ghana and East Africa: Pan-Africanism and Interstate Relations*, Madison, New Jersey, USA: Fairleigh Dickinson University Press, 1992, p. 152).

Félix Houphouët-Boigny, president of the Ivory Coast who was hostile towards Nkrumah as much as he was towards Sékou Touré, also said the coup against Nkrumah was externally engineered. As he stated in an interview with *Jeune Afrique*, 4 February 1981:

"Destabilisation is not a new thing. Did you know why Idi Amin made his coup in 1972? (1971). It was not he who did it, but the British. He did not even know what he wanted himself.

It was the same in Ghana when the military overthrew Nkrumah. They [the Ghanaian coup makers] came to see me. I asked them why. They replied: 'All is not well anymore.' 'Is that all?' [I asked them]. I also asked them what they were going to do; they did not know. People outside knew it for them."

In the case of Nyerere, his credentials as an uncompromising supporter of the liberation struggle in Africa were solidified by the contribution he and his country made for decades towards the attainment of freedom and independence in the countries of southern Africa which were still under white minority rule including the bastion, and citadel, of white supremacy on the continent: apartheid South Africa.

The sacrifices Tanzania – under the leadership of Nyerere - made during the liberation struggle in southern Africa will always be remembered even if they are overlooked or ignored by some of the people we helped. One example of the contributions Tanzania made to the liberation struggle was explained by a British journalist, David Martin, after he interviewed Nyerere one day:

"I remember one day sitting in his office questioning that a number of African countries had not paid their subscriptions to the OAU Liberation Committee Special Fund for the Liberation of Africa.

He looked at me for some moments, thoughtfully chewing the inside corner of his mouth in his distinctive way. Then, his decision made, he passed across a file swearing me secrecy as to its contents.

It contained the amount that Tanzanians, then according to the United Nations the poorest people on earth, would directly and indirectly contribute that year to the liberation movements. I was astounded; the amount ran into millions of US dollars.

It was the practice among national leaders in those days to say that their countries did not have guerrilla bases. Now we know that Tanzania had many such bases providing training for most of the southern African guerrillas, who were then called 'terrorists' and who today are members of governments throughout the region....

Tanzania was also directly attacked from Mozambique by the Portuguese. But, in turn, each of the white minorities in southern Africa fell to black majority political rule and Nyerere saw his vision for the continent finally realized on 27 April 1994 when apartheid formally ended in South Africa with the swearing in of a new black leadership." - (David Martin, "A Candle on Kilimanjaro," in *Southern African Features*, 21 December 2001).

Then there was the enormous sacrifice Tanzania made in the liberation wars in terms of lives. She lost soldiers, men and women, so that others could live and win their freedom. They did. All that was done because of Nyerere. As President Yoweri Museveni said about Nyerere:

"He was the greatest black man that ever lived. There are other black men such as Nelson Mandela and Kwame Nkrumah, but Nyerere was the greatest." - (Yoweri Museveni, quoted by *New Vision*, Kampala, 4 April 2012).

Nkrumah also stands out in more than one way. He blazed the trail for the African independence movement when he led the Gold Coast to become the first black African country to emerge from colonial rule. He was also in a class by himself in his quest for immediate continental unification and will always be. There will never be another Nkrumah.

And both Nkrumah and Nyerere pursued their goals relentlessly and at an enormous cost to themselves and their countries, although they did not succeed in convincing their colleagues to unite their countries under one government.

It is for future generations of Africans to decide if they want Africa to unite.

9 781724 755674